Numeracy Pupil's Book

Year 6

Peter Patilla &
Paul Broadbent

EDUCATIONAL

Every effort has been made to trace copyright holders and to obtain their permission for the use of copyright material. The authors and publishers will gladly receive information enabling them to rectify any error or omission in subsequent editions.

First published 1999

Letts Educational, Schools and Colleges Division, 9–15 Aldine Street, London
W12 8AW
Tel: (020) 8740 2270
Fax: (020) 8740 2280

Text © Peter Patilla and Paul Broadbent
Editorial, design and production © Gecko Limited, Bicester, Oxon
Illustrations © Peter and Janet Simmonett, except Jan Nesbitt: p. 64;
David Pattison: p. 14; Peter Richardson: pp. 34, 48; Jake Tebbit: pp. 24, 82;
Andy Warrington: pp. 16, 62.
Cover illustration © Beccy Blake.

British Library Cataloguing-in-Publication Data
A CIP record for this book is available from the British Library.

ISBN 1 84085 276 3
Printed and bound in Spain
Letts Educational is the trading name of BPP [Letts Educational] Ltd

CONTENTS

Do you remember?

1 What percentage is the same as $\frac{1}{4}$?

    a 40%   **b** 25%   **c** 50%   **d** 75%

2 What is the total of 600 ml and 1.25 l?

    a 1850 ml   **b** 1625 ml   **c** 16 025 ml   **d** 1805 ml

3 Which of these numbers is *not* a factor of 36?

    a 12   **b** 4   **c** 8   **d** 9

4 How many lines of symmetry has this shape?

    a 1   **b** 2   **c** 3   **d** 4

5 What time is this in 12-hour time?

    a 1.35   **b** 5.35   **c** 4.25   **d** 3.35

6 What is 10% of £4?

   a 4p   **b** £3.60   **c** £3.90   **d** 40p

7 What is the mode for this set of temperatures?

17 °C   16 °C   14 °C   17 °C   14 °C   15 °C   14 °C   13 °C   15 °C

   a 13 °C   **b** 14 °C   **c** 15 °C   **d** 16 °C

8 What is 0.4 as a fraction?

   a $\frac{2}{5}$ **b** $\frac{1}{4}$ **c** $\frac{4}{5}$ **d** $\frac{2}{10}$

9 What is the area of this rectangle?

9 cm

7 cm

   a 32 cm²   **b** 81 cm²   **c** 63 cm²   **d** 49 cm²

10 What sort of triangle is this?

   a equilateral   **b** isosceles   **c** right-angled   **d** scalene

Check your answers on page 96. ✓

Place value

100	200	300	400	500	600	700	800	900
10	20	30	40	50	60	70	80	90
1	2	3	4	5	6	7	8	9
0.1	0.2	0.3	0.4	0.5	0.6	0.7	0.8	0.9
0.01	0.02	0.03	0.04	0.05	0.06	0.07	0.08	0.09
0.001	0.002	0.003	0.004	0.005	0.006	0.007	0.008	0.009

Starters

Answer these.

1   0.7×10
2   $0.0.4 \times 100$
3   0.6×100
4   0.003×100
5   0.005×1000
6   $1 \div 1000$
7   $60 \div 100$
8   $400 \div 1000$
9   $0.3 \div 100$
10 $0.09 \div 10$

Practice

A Write the value of the red digit.

1 3.6**1**	**2** 8**5**031	**3** 0.7**4**3	**4** 37.04**9**
5 **6**20 039	**6** 1**7**3.05	**7** 3 **9**00 470	**8** 1.0**3**4
9 7396.0**4**	**10** 16.4**8**9	**11** 3 **1**00 000	**12** 0.0**0**1

B Write the decimal numbers shown by each arrow.

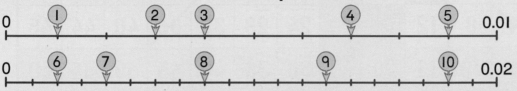

C Multiply each of these by 10.

1 3.7	**2** 1.81	**3** 0.03	**4** 17.62
5 102.8	**6** 7.05	**7** 10.03	**8** 0.14

Multiply each of these by 100.

9 7.23	**10** 1.05	**11** 0.61	**12** 14.09
13 0.316	**14** 7.205	**15** 11.094	**16** 2.171

D Divide each of these by 10.

1 714	**2** 1538	**3** 21.9	**4** 16.5
5 0.35	**6** 7.02	**7** 19.48	**8** 30.25

Divide each of these by 100.

9 16.3	**10** 1847	**11** 30.5	**12** 61 430
13 428.6	**14** 0.7	**15** 2.3	**16** 37.9

Challenge

Set up a ÷10 constant on your calculator.

Look at the pattern.

Change the 3 to a
different starting number.

1 0 ÷ ÷ 1 0 = 3 = = =

Multiplication and division

×	1	2	3	4	5	6	7	8	9	10	11	12
1	1	2	3	4	5	6	7	8	9	10	11	12
2	2	4	6	8	10	12	14	16	18	20	22	24
3	3	6	9	12	15	18	21	24	27	30	33	36
4	4	8	12	16	20	24	28	32	36	40	44	48
5	5	10	15	20	25	30	35	40	45	50	55	60
6	6	12	18	24	30	36	42	48	54	60	66	72
7	7	14	21	28	35	42	49	56	63	70	77	84
8	8	16	24	32	40	48	56	64	72	80	88	96
9	9	18	27	36	45	54	63	72	81	90	99	108
10	10	20	30	40	50	60	70	80	90	100	110	110
11	11	22	33	44	55	66	77	88	99	110	121	132
12	12	24	36	48	60	72	84	96	108	120	132	144

Starters

Answer these.

1 6×7 2 4×8 3 11×4 4 12×7 5 8×9

6 11×12 7 $77 \div 11$ 8 $54 \div 9$ 9 $108 \div 12$ 10 $144 \div 12$

11 $56 \div 7$ 12 $48 \div 8$

Practice

A Answer these.

1	40 × 90	2	30 × 70	3	50 × 80	4	60 × 30
5	80 × 90	6	540 ÷ 60	7	270 ÷ 30	8	800 ÷ 80
9	360 ÷ 60	10	420 ÷ 70	11	0.7 × 20	12	0.3 × 40
13	0.6 × 50	14	0.8 × 90	15	0.4 × 70	16	36 ÷ 60
17	18 ÷ 30	18	54 ÷ 90	19	28 ÷ 40	20	32 ÷ 80

B Copy and complete the tables.

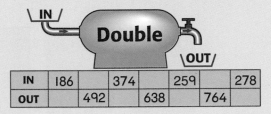

IN	186		374		259		278
OUT		492		638		764	

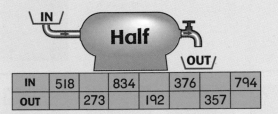

IN	518		834		376		794
OUT		273		192		357	

C Use halving and doubling to help answer these.

1	8 × 32	2	16 × 15	3	17 × 12	4	37 × 25
5	300 ÷ 12	6	250 ÷ 20	7	700 ÷ 40	8	800 ÷ 16
9	14 × 32	10	35 × 50	11	24 × 19	12	82 × 16

D Find all the different products you can make using pairs of these.

0.4 **1.6** **0.02** **1.5** **0.9**

Challenge

Use any of these eight numbers to make the target number.   **Target: 3094**

Use each number once only.
You can use brackets.

Make up your own target number game.

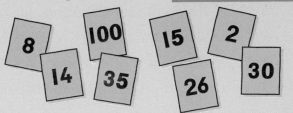

8 100 15 2 14 35 26 30

Multiplication

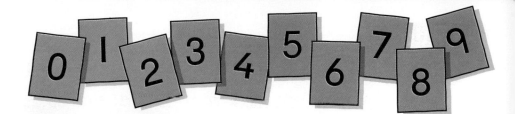

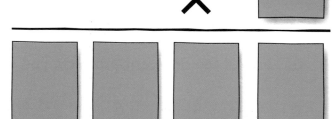

Starters

Use digit cards.

1 Write 10 different multiplications for the red sum.
2 Write a rule for not getting five digits in the answer.
3 Write 10 different multiplications for the green sum.
4 Write a rule for getting three digits before the decimal point.

10

Practice

A

1	2	3	4	5
5143	8615	9052	4813	7174
× 4	× 3	× 6	× 5	× 6

6	7	8	9	10
8149	4806	1095	3129	4683
× 3	× 7	× 8	× 9	× 6

B Calculate the areas of each of these rectangles.

1 43 cm
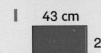 29 cm

2 19 cm
32 cm

3 34 cm
21 cm

4 72 cm
68 cm

5 61 cm
38 cm

6 18 cm
 19 cm

7 46 cm
39 cm

C

1	2	3	4	5
73.6	49.5	87.6	29.8	31.6
× 4	× 8	× 3	× 5	× 9

6	7	8	9	10
8.53	5.87	9.68	34.85	29.37
× 7	× 4	× 8	× 6	× 5

D What is the total cost of:

1 3 pens and 4 pencil sharpeners

2 4 calculators and 5 pens

3 2 of each item

 £6.49

 £3.74

 £1.58

Challenge

Multiply 37037 **by different numbers.**

Investigate the number patterns made by the products.

Decimals

0.35	1.045	0.328	2.06
1.93	0.09	2.72	1.452
0.009	2.75	0.05	1.178
0.25	1.02	0.33	0.908

Starters

Look at the decimal numbers on the grid.

1 Which is the largest decimal?

2 Which is the smallest decimal?

3 Which decimal is equivalent to $\frac{1}{4}$?

4 Which decimal is equivalent to $\frac{9}{100}$?

5 Which decimal is nearest to 1?

6 Which decimal is half of 0.7?

7 Write the numbers that are less than 1.

8 the numbers that are less than 0.1.

9 Which two decimals total 3?

10 Which two decimals have a difference of 0.3?

Practice

A What does the digit 4 represent in each of these?

1 46.3	2 6.942	3 0.041	4 8.324	5 7.403	6 0.004
7 52.4	8 84.9	9 1.045	10 3.74	11 6.481	12 3.04

B Write the decimal numbers these arrows point to.

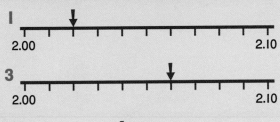

1. (number line from 2.00 to 2.10, arrow pointing near 2.02)

2. (number line from 2.00 to 2.10, arrow pointing near 2.09)

3. (number line from 2.00 to 2.10, arrow pointing near 2.05)

4. (number line from 5.000 to 5.010, arrow pointing near 5.001)

5. (number line from 5.000 to 5.010, arrow pointing near 5.003)

6. (number line from 5.000 to 5.010, arrow pointing near 5.008)

C Write these in order, starting with the smallest

3.05   3.51   3.115   3.14   3.7   3.283

0.75   0.075   0.7   0.699   0.024   0.3

2.5 m   0.52 m   5.02 m   2.05 m   5.2 m   0.25 m

1.75 kg   1.075 kg   1.7 kg   1.05 kg   1.57 kg

Challenge

Use cards the same as these. Arrange all the cards to make numbers.

1   4   8   5

1 Which is the largest number?
2 Which is the smallest?
3 Which is the number nearest to 5?
4 Write all the numbers in order, starting with the smallest.
5 Try the activity again with four different digits.

Percentages, ratio and proportion

What percentage of the fish are:

1 red?
2 blue?
3 green?
4 yellow?

What proportion of the creatures are:

5 fish?
6 starfish?
7 crabs?

Practice

A **Change these test scores to percentages.**

1 $\frac{4}{10}$ 2 $\frac{17}{20}$ 3 $\frac{17}{25}$ 4 $\frac{13}{20}$

5 $\frac{3}{4}$ 6 $\frac{45}{50}$ 7 $\frac{3}{5}$ 8 $\frac{7}{10}$

Now write the scores in order, starting with the lowest percentage.

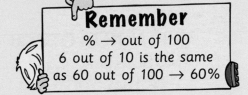

Remember

% → out of 100
6 out of 10 is the same
as 60 out of 100 → 60%

B **Copy and complete these equivalents.**

percentage	46%		35%			90%		74%			30%	
decimal		0.25		0.7			0.32			0.95		0.52
fraction	$\frac{23}{50}$	$\frac{1}{4}$			$\frac{1}{5}$				$\frac{9}{20}$			

C **Answer these.**

1 10% of 30 2 20% of 50 3 25% of 16 4 10% of 80 5 1% of 200

6 50% of 16 7 25% of 80 8 20% of 10 9 1% of 500 10 5% of 40

D **Some red and blue marbles were put in a bag.**
The ratio of red to blue marbles was 2 red to every 3 blue.

Copy and complete this table.

Red marbles	2	4				32
Blue marbles	3		15			
Total	5			20	35	

Challenge

Draw a 5 × 4 grid on squared paper.

Use two colours to make a pattern.
What is the ratio of the two colours?

Investigate other possible ratios using two colours.

Handling data

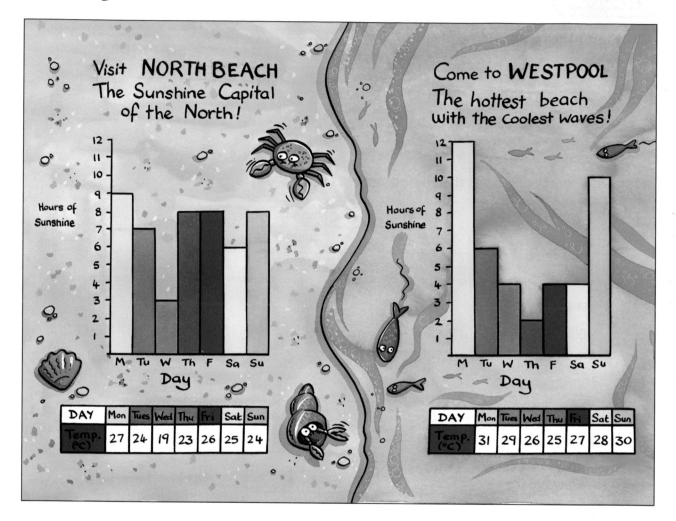

Visit **NORTH BEACH**
The Sunshine Capital
of the North!

DAY	Mon	Tues	Wed	Thu	Fri	Sat	Sun
Temp. (°C)	27	24	19	23	26	25	24

Come to **WESTPOOL**
The hottest beach
with the coolest waves!

DAY	Mon	Tues	Wed	Thu	Fri	Sat	Sun
Temp. (°C)	31	29	26	25	27	28	30

Starters

Answer these.

1 How many more hours of sunshine were there in Westpool than in North Beach on Monday?

2 What was the difference in temperature between the resorts on Friday?

3 What was the range of temperature in each resort for the week?

4 What is the median temperature for each resort for the week?

Practice

A These are the heights,
to the nearest centimetre,
of a group of sunflowers
planted by some children.

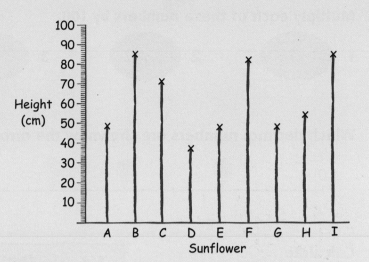

1 Write the heights in order,
starting with the shortest.

2 What is the range?

3 What is the median height?

4 What is the mode?

5 What is the mean height?

B Some trees were planted in a park.
This graph shows the heights
of the trees in centimetres.

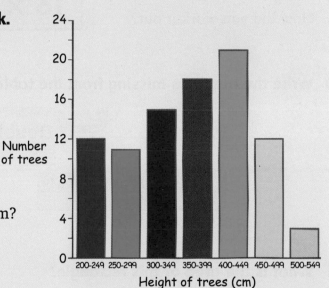

1 How many trees were between
350 cm and 399 cm in height?

2 How many trees were greater
than 400 cm in height?

3 How many more trees were
between 400 cm and 449 cm
than between 200 cm and 249 cm?

4 How many trees were planted
altogether?

Challenge

Cut out card squares and draw the diagonals.
Colour the quarters in different ways.
Predict the probability of landing on each
of the colours on your spinner.
Spin the spinner 100 times and record your results.

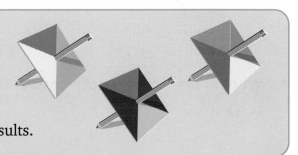

  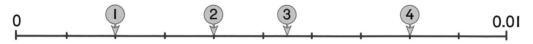

Review

A Multiply each of these numbers by 100.

1 **1.473**   2 **0.687**   3 **31.8**   4 **147.85**

B Which decimal numbers are shown by the arrows?

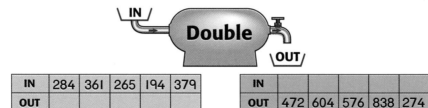

C Calculate

How did you work it out?

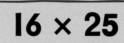
16 × 25

D Write the numbers missing from the tables.

Double

IN	284	361	265	194	379
OUT					

IN					
OUT	472	604	576	838	274

E What is the area of this rectangle?

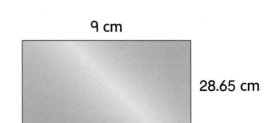

9 cm

28.65 cm

F What is the approximate answer to:

Work it out.

3897 × 6 ?

G Write these in order starting with the smallest.

| 1.805 | 1.72 | 1.9 | 1.85 | 1.815 | 1.795 | 1.095 |

H Change these to improper fractions.

1 $3\frac{2}{5}$ 2 $8\frac{3}{10}$ 3 $5\frac{2}{3}$ 4 $6\frac{3}{8}$

I   Which of these is not the same as $\frac{1}{4}$?

| 25% | $\frac{25}{100}$ | 0.4 | 0.25 | $\frac{3}{12}$ |

J   What is 20% of 40?

K Talk about ratio:

L What is the mode, median and mean of this set of numbers?

6 8 2 4 3 6 8 3 5 8 2

Quadrilaterals

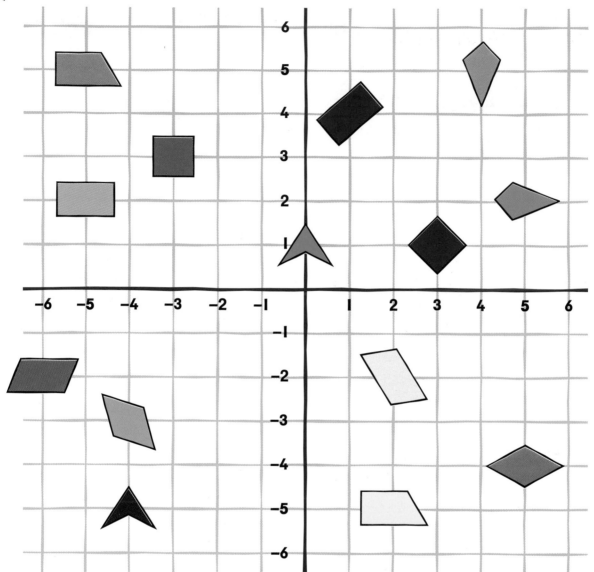

Starters

Write the co-ordinates for each of these shapes:

1 kite

2 arrowhead

3 rhombus

Which shapes are at the following co-ordinates?

4 (−6, −2)

5 (−3, 3)

6 (2, −5)

Practice

A **Draw this Carroll diagram.**

Sort these quadrilaterals on the diagram.

rectangle

square

rhombus

trapezium

kite

arrow head

parallelogram

	parallel sides	not parallel sides
right angled		
not right angled		

B **Which of these shapes has been rotated?**

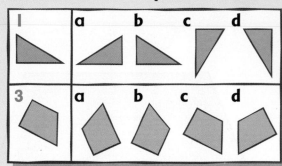

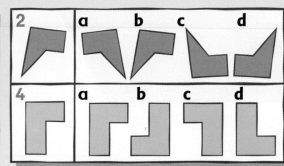

C **True or false?**

1 A rhombus is a special parallelogram.

2 The angles of a quadrilateral add up to 180°.

3 A trapezium has a pair of parallel sides.

4 Opposite angles of a rhombus are equal.

5 A parallelogram has two lines of symmetry.

Challenge

Design a tessellating tile

1 Cut out a shape from a square of card.

2 Move the cut-out piece across and tape it together.

3 Draw round your shape tile to make a tessellated pattern.
Try starting with other shapes.

Measuring perimeters

1 Measure the perimeter of each shape.   Write about anything you notice.
2 Measure the diagonals of each shape.

Practice

A Fencing costs £9 per metre.

What is the cost of putting fencing around each of these gardens?

 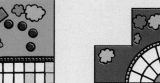 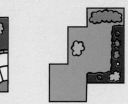 

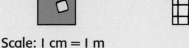

Scale: 1 cm = 1 m

B Copy and complete.

1 3.45 m = ⬜ cm	**2** 6.815 km = ⬜ m	**3** 1.3 m = ⬜ mm
4 8.425 km = ⬜ m	**5** 0.7 cm = ⬜ mm	**6** 0.82 m = ⬜ cm
7 0.455 km = ⬜ m	**8** 0.26 m = ⬜ mm	**9** 750 m = ⬜ km
10 6 cm = ⬜ m	**11** 146 cm = ⬜ m	**12** 27 mm = ⬜ cm

C Find the equivalence between metric and imperial lengths:

inch   foot
metre   millimetre
    yard   kilometre
centimetre   mile

Metric → Imperial
1 cm → ⬜ inch

Imperial → Metric
1 inch → ⬜ cm

Challenge

Tricky measures

How could you find:
- the thickness of a piece of paper?
- the distance from your school to Paris?
- the distance stretched arm to arm for all the children in your school?

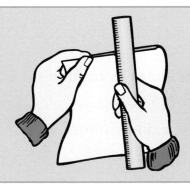

23

World times

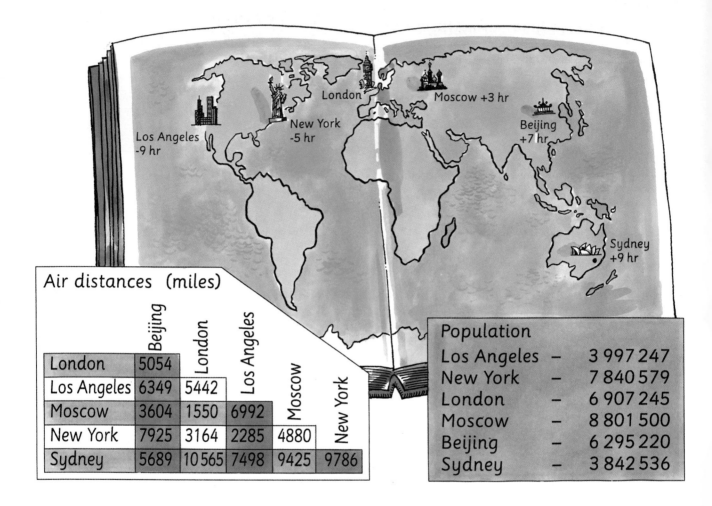

Air distances (miles)

	Beijing	London	Los Angeles	Moscow	New York
London	5054				
Los Angeles	6349	5442			
Moscow	3604	1550	6992		
New York	7925	3164	2285	4880	
Sydney	5689	10565	7498	9425	9786

Population
Los Angeles – 3 997 247
New York – 7 840 579
London – 6 907 245
Moscow – 8 801 500
Beijing – 6 295 220
Sydney – 3 842 536

Starters

1 Write the cities in population order, starting with the smallest.

2 How far is it from Moscow to Los Angeles?

Write the times in London for each of these:

3 4.15 p.m. in Moscow.

4 7.30 a.m. in New York.

5 2.10 p.m. in Beijing.

Practice

A Write these times using 12-hr and 24-hr notation.

| 6:15 p.m. | 18:15 |

morning
1 6.35 2 7.08
3 9.48 4 11.26

afternoon
5 1.05 6 2.37
7 4.26 8 5.03

evening
9 7.55 10 9.13
11 10.47 12 11.22

B Complete this table of cooking times.

Turkey must be cooked for 60 minutes for every kg.

Chicken must be cooked for 50 minutes for every kg.

kilograms	1	1.5	2	2.5	3	3.5
Cooking time in minutes (turkey)						
Cooking time in minutes (chicken)						

C Round each measurement to the nearest tenth of a unit.

1 3750 cm ≈ ☐ m

2 4814 mm ≈ ☐ cm

3 6848 m ≈ ☐ km

4 9235 cm ≈ ☐ m

Round each measurement to the nearest whole unit.

5 2613 mm ≈ ☐ cm

6 4146 m ≈ ☐ km

7 3508 cm ≈ ☐ m

8 2493 m ≈ ☐ km

Challenge

Measure the circumference and diameter of each coin, to the nearest millimetre.

Money problems

STATEMENT DATE	31 December 1999			STATEMENT NUMBER	1 of 3

NUMBER   0294873625957

Date	Details	Withdrawals (£)	Deposits (£)	Balance (£)
7.8.99	Open account		125.00	125.00
15.8.99	Cash		34.00	159.00
1.9.99	Cheque		85.49	244.49
3.10.99	Cash	60.00		184.49
22.10.99	Cash	45.00		
13.11.99	Cheque		134.85	
27.11.99	Cheque		76.30	
15.12.99	Cash	125.00		

Starters

Calculate the balance for each of these dates:

1 22.10.99   **2** 13.11.99   **3** 27.11.99   **4** 15.12.99

Practice

A Answer these.

1 $58 + 93$	2 $65 + 83$	3 $94 + 87$	4 $174 + 39$
5 $384 + 58$	6 $614 + 69$	7 $441 + 384$	8 $815 + 293$
9 $96 - 58$	10 $84 - 37$	11 $97 - 43$	12 $514 - 88$
13 $637 - 94$	14 $284 - 78$	15 $593 - 284$	16 $420 - 168$

B Total each set

1  2  3 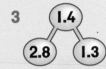 4 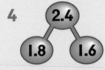 5

2.5
1.9 1.5

C Copy and complete.

1 $1900 - 170 = \boxed{}$

$8600 - \boxed{} = 5960$

$\boxed{} - 380 = 8920$

$1800 - 40 = \boxed{}$

$\boxed{} - 360 = 4794$

2 $7000 - 140 = \boxed{}$

$14\,000 - \boxed{} = 13\,997$

$\boxed{} - 50 = 79\,950$

$23\,000 - 60 = \boxed{}$

$49\,000 - \boxed{} = 48\,992$

3 $4002 - 1994 = \boxed{}$

$6003 - \boxed{} = 800$

$\boxed{} - 6995 = 90$

$5004 - 499 = \boxed{}$

$8008 - \boxed{} = 60$

D Answer these.

1	2	3	4	5
$\begin{array}{r} 1485 \\ +\ 2746 \\ \hline \end{array}$	$\begin{array}{r} 6148 \\ +\ 3794 \\ \hline \end{array}$	$\begin{array}{r} 4807 \\ +\ 6394 \\ \hline \end{array}$	$\begin{array}{r} 9027 \\ -\ 3854 \\ \hline \end{array}$	$\begin{array}{r} 4705 \\ -\ 1816 \\ \hline \end{array}$

6	7	8	9	10
$\begin{array}{r} 6004 \\ -\ 1937 \\ \hline \end{array}$	$\begin{array}{r} 148.70 \\ +\ 37.85 \\ \hline \end{array}$	$\begin{array}{r} 294.38 \\ +184.80 \\ \hline \end{array}$	$\begin{array}{r} 21.63 \\ -\ 9.84 \\ \hline \end{array}$	$\begin{array}{r} 161.05 \\ -\ 93.61 \\ \hline \end{array}$

Challenge

Find all the different totals you can make by using three of these five numbers.

1.84   21.7   8.1   1.52   9.3

Number sequences

A

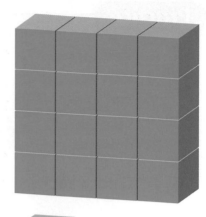

B

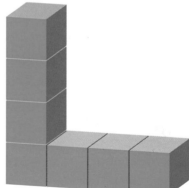

C

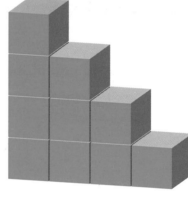

1 What are row A called?

2 What are row B called?

3 What are row C called?

Investigate any patterns you notice with them.

Practice

A Copy and continue each sequence.

1	17	26	35	44	___	___	___	___
2	124	99	74	49	___	___	___	___
3	0.2	0.4	0.6	0.8	___	___	___	___
4	27	19	11	3	___	___	___	___
5	0.25	0.5	0.75	1.0	___	___	___	___

B List all the factors you know for each number.

  1 48   **2** 30   **3** 27   **4** 32   **5** 60   **6** 100

C 1 What will be the next number of rods in these sequences?

  2 Write a formula for each sequence.

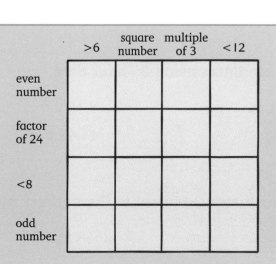

D Write these in full.

  1 8^2 **2** 6^2 **3** 10^2 **4** 15^2 **5** 9^2 **6** 1^2 **7** 100^2 **8** 50^2

Challenge

Write the numbers 1 to 16 on pieces of paper.

Place them on the grid so that they follow the rules.

Copy the grid and numbers when you have finished.

	>6	square number	multiple of 3	<12
even number				
factor of 24				
<8				
odd number				

Review

A Name each type of quadrilateral.

1  2 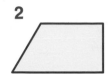 3   4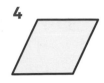

B Write the co-ordinates for the vertices of the triangle.

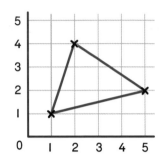

C Measure accurately to find the perimeter of this shape.

D 1 0.665 km = ☐ m   2 1.6 m = ☐ mm   3 18 cm = ☐ m

E Write these times using 24-hour time.

1 2.34 p.m.   2 8.15 a.m.   3 6.55 p.m.

4 10.08 p.m.   5 11.48 a.m.

F Round each measurement to the nearest whole unit.

1 3418 cm ≈ ☐ m   2 2649 mm ≈ ☐ cm   3 2503 m ≈ ☐ km

G Total these.

1 2.9   4.8   3.6

2 6.1   0.7   3.8

H

1
```
  1 3 4 . 8 4
+   9 7 . 3 9
-------------
```

2
```
  2 0 7 . 3 1
+ 1 6 2 . 9 3
-------------
```

I

1
```
  4 0 3 . 6 2
-   8 7 . 3 9
-------------
```

2
```
  6 2 7 . 0 4
- 1 3 8 . 1 2
-------------
```

J What are the missing numbers?

1 1 ☐ ☐ 16 ☐ 36 49

2 1 3 ☐ ☐ ☐ 21 28

K What is the square of:

1 8   2 12   3 20   4 30

L Continue each sequence.

1 3.75   3.5   3.25   3.0   __ __ __ __

2 1.7   1.9   2.1   2.3   __ __ __ __

Do you remember?

1 **What is the value of the red digit.**

a 8 thousands   **b** 8 hundredths

c 8 thousandths   **d** 8 tenths

62.3**18**

---

2 **Which decimal number could this be:**

$$1.36 > \boxed{?} > 1.3$$

a 1.39   **b** 1.4   **c** 1.32   **d** 1.29

---

3 **What is the area of this rectangle?**

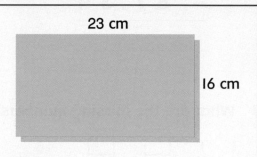

23 cm

16 cm

a 368 cm²   **b** 78 cm²   **c** 184 cm²   **d** 39 cm²

---

4 **What is this as an improper fraction?**

$4\frac{3}{5}$

a $\frac{20}{5}$ **b** $\frac{7}{5}$ **c** $\frac{2}{30}$ **d** $\frac{23}{5}$

---

5 **What is $\frac{2}{5}$ as a percentage?**

a 20%   **b** 50%   **c** 40%   **d** 80%

6 **What is the median value of this set of numbers?**

16   24   13   37   22   17   19   27   31

a 22   **b** 27   **c** 24   **d** 31

---

7 **How many lines of symmetry has a parallelogram?**

a 4   **b** 2   **c** 1   **d** 0

---

8 **If the area of this square is 144 cm², what is the perimeter?**

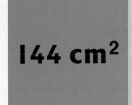

144 cm²

a 62 cm   **b** 48 cm   **c** 52 cm   **d** 42 cm

---

9 **If the time is 0953, what is the time in 3 hrs 10 mins?**

a 1243   **b** 0103   **c** 1303   **d** 1203

---

10 **What is the next number in this sequence?**   64   49   36   25   ☐

a 15   **b** 9   **c** 12   **d** 16

Check your answers on page 96. ✓

Negative numbers

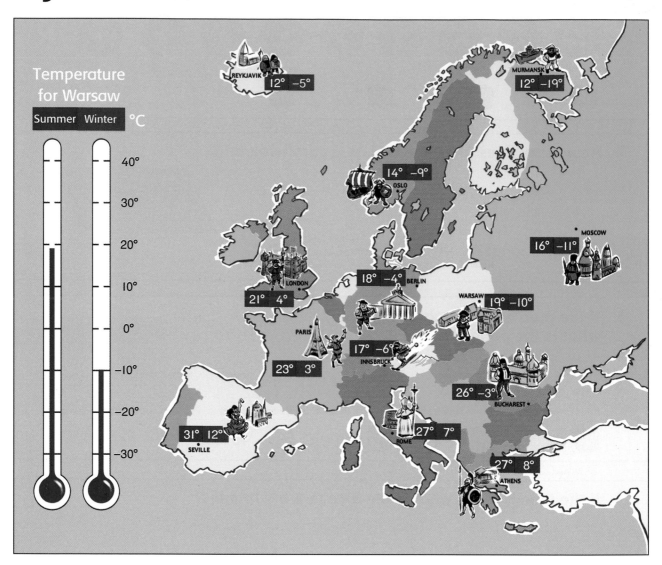

Starters

What is the difference between summer temperature and winter temperature in:

1 Moscow   **2** Bucharest   **3** Berlin   **4** Murmansk   **5** Oslo

Write the cities in order of winter temperature, starting with the lowest temperature.

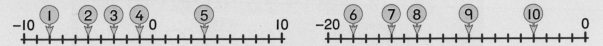

Practice

A Write the numbers which the arrows point to.

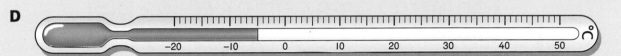

B Put each set of numbers in order, negative numbers first.

1 −8 4 6 −3 3 1 −17 −4

2 3 −9 −3 −17 −6 −4 −1 1

3 −7 −6 −4 −1 14 −19 3 2

C Copy and complete each number pattern.

1 14 9 4 __ __ __ __   2 20 11 2 __ __ __ __

3 17 11 5 __ __ __ __   4 9 7 5 __ __ __ __

5 −15 −9 −3 __ __ __ __   6 −11 −7 −3 __ __ __ __

D

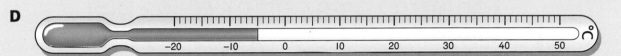

1 What is the temperature on the thermometer?

2 If the temperature rises by 6 °C, what is the new temperature?

3 If the temperature falls by 7 °C, what is the new temperature?

4 By how much does the temperature have to rise to show 10 °C?

5 If the temperature is 3 °C, by how much has it risen?

Challenge

Set up a 'minus' constant on your calculator.

change the [4] for a different start number

change the [1] for a different step.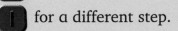

35

Brackets

0	1	2	3	4	5	6	7	8	9
10	11	12	13	14	15	16	17	18	19
20	21	22	23	24	25	26	27	28	29
30	31	32	33	34	35	36	37	38	39
40	41	42	43	44	45	46	47	48	49
50	51	52	53	54	55	56	57	58	59
60	61	62	63	64	65	66	67	68	69
70	71	72	73	74	75	76	77	78	79
80	81	82	83	84	85	86	87	88	89
90	91	92	93	94	95	96	97	98	99

Starters

Play 'Square Deal'
– a game for 2 or more players.

You need: counters, digit cards 0–9.

Player 1 shuffles the cards and turns over the top 3 numbers.

Player 1 uses these to make a number on the grid, and covers the number with a coloured counter on the grid.

Player 2 then takes a turn.

The first to make a 'square' of numbers, e.g. is the winner.

12	13
22	23

For example:

 ⟹

$37 \times 2 = 74$

$(7 - 3) \times 2 = 2$

$(2 + 3) \times 7 = 35$

$(7 \times 2) \ 3 = 42$

$7 + 3 + 2 = 12$

$27 \div 3 = 9$

Practice

A Answer these.

1 (6 × 4) + 5
2 18 − (32 ÷ 4)
3 8 × (22 − 15)
4 (38 + 6) ÷ 6
5 320 − (70 × 4)
6 (190 − 65) ÷ 5
7 (8 × 3) + (36 ÷ 6)
8 (120 + 45) ÷ (18 − 13)
9 (37 + 9) − (180 ÷ 9)

B Copy these, adding brackets to make each sum true.

1 4 × 8 + 3 = 44
2 57 − 6 × 7 = 15
3 14 + 8 ÷ 8 + 3 = 2
4 8 × 5 − 3 + 9 = 28
5 64 ÷ 8 × 4 = 32
6 43 + 9 × 6 = 97
7 4 × 7 + 30 = 58
8 19 + 17 ÷ 14 − 8 = 6
9 17 + 18 − 6 × 4 = 11

C Copy these, adding brackets to make each sum true.

1 37 − 4 × 7 = 23 + 13 ÷ 4
2 56 ÷ 7 + 1 = 42 ÷ 6 + 2
3 38 − 15 + 7 = 40 − 3 × 8
4 9 + 6 × 3 = 2 + 5 × 5

D Answer these.

1 12 × 15
2 16 × 32
3 35 × 18
4 13 × 51
5 17 × 19
6 18 × 99
7 9.3 × 7
8 4.8 × 8
9 6.2 × 4
10 9.1 × 8
11 7.6 × 4
12 8.5 × 6

E Answer these. What could the missing number be?

1 306 ÷ 18 = 306 ÷ ☐ ÷ 6
2 777 ÷ 21 = 777 ÷ ☐ ÷ 3
3 456 ÷ 24 = 456 ÷ ☐ ÷ ☐
4 425 ÷ 25 = 425 ÷ ☐ ÷ ☐

Challenge

Use the digits 1 to 6 once in the boxes to make the statement true.

Make up other puzzles like this.

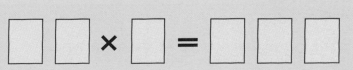

Division

$$8 \overline{\smash{\big)}\ \square\,\square\square\!.\,\square}$$

$$8 \overline{\smash{\big)}\ \square\square\!.\,\square}$$

$$8 \overline{\smash{\big)}\ \square\!.\,\square\square}$$

Starters

Write three division sums for each type.

Practice

A Work these out in your head.

1 70 × 300	2 900 × 50	3 255 × 2	4 410 × 2
5 900 × 7	6 40 × 60	7 83 × 5	8 6 × 34
9 20 × 8.6	10 80 × 1.2	11 4.2 × 200	12 0.3 × 600
13 8.3 × 100	14 0.75 × 200	15 6.2 × 4	16 8.5 × 3

B Work out the missing numbers.

1 ☐ ÷ 100 = 47   2 ☐ ÷ 10 = 18.5   3 ☐ ÷ 1000 = 0.63

4 247 ÷ ☐ = 2.47   5 3.8 ÷ ☐ = 0.38   6 17.5 ÷ ☐ = 0.175

7 843 ÷ 100 = ☐   8 95.2 ÷ 100 = ☐   9 764 ÷ 1000 = ☐

C Which digits are hidden? Use digits 1–8 to complete these.

1	2	3	4
●●	●74	91	142
6 ⟌ 210	4 ⟌ 69●	8 ⟌ 7●●	● ⟌ 99●

D Calculate these.

1 952 ÷ 28	2 703 ÷ 19	3 918 ÷ 34	4 988 ÷ 26
5 936 ÷ 24	6 666 ÷ 18	7 912 ÷ 16	8 774 ÷ 43
9 838 ÷ 27	10 479 ÷ 21	11 638 ÷ 42	12 916 ÷ 38

Challenge

The missing numbers in these divisions are consecutive.

Work out what they are.

1224 ÷ ☐ ÷ ☐ = 17   1092 ÷ ☐ ÷ ☐ = 6   3808 ÷ ☐ ÷ ☐ = 14

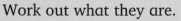

Make up some puzzles like this using consecutive numbers.

Money problems

Holidays in America

Flights:
Adult £217 return
Child £147 return

Hotel
(£) per night
Adult: 48
Child: 29

Car Hire
($) per week
Small family: 95
Large family: 138
Luxury: 184

Adventure Land
Day tickets
Family ticket: $120
(2 adults/2 children)
Adult ticket: $38
Children's ticket: $27

£1 (pound sterling) = $1.50 (dollars)
$1 (dollar) = £0.66 (pound sterling)

Starters

Answer these.

1 How much would it cost for 2 adults and 1 child to stay at the hotel for 9 nights?

2 What is the total cost of the flight for 2 adults and 2 children?

3 How much more expensive is the luxury car than the large family car over 2 weeks, in dollars and in pounds?

4 A family of 2 adults and 2 children want to stay 6 nights at the hotel, and visit Adventure Land. Including the flight, will this be less than £1300, which is the amount they have to spend on a holiday?

Practice

A Answer these.

1 The Empire cinema has 420 seats. How many tickets are sold if all the seats are filled every night for a fortnight?

2 A ream of paper is 500 sheets. There are 5 reams in a box. How many sheets is this?

3 If a sheet of paper weighs 2.5 g, what is the weight of a box of paper?

4 248 children and 34 adults went on a school trip. Buses seat 57 people. How many buses were needed?

5 There is space in the multi-storey car park for 16 rows of 40 cars on each of 6 floors. How many cars can park?

6 Sam needs a score of 123 in darts. He throws a 20, a double 16 and a double 17. What score does he now need?

7 Andy the window cleaner works 8-hour days. If he averages 2 houses each hour, how many houses will he have visited in 6 days?

8 In a dance there are 2 boys and 3 girls in every line. 48 girls take part in the dance. How many boys take part?

B Starline Railway Company offers these discounts for block bookings:

Number of seats	Discount (money off)
20–50	£1 per passenger
51–100	£2 per passenger
over 100	£3 per passenger

Work out the cost of these bookings:

1 22 seats at £16 each   2 34 seats at £47 each   3 58 seats at £19 each

4 87 seats at £28 each   5 135 seats at £37 each   6 200 seats at £18.50 each

Challenge

In the USA they still use feet and inches.

- How many feet is the perimeter of your classroom?
- How many inches is the perimeter of your desk?

Find the equivalences for:

feet ⟷ metres

inches ⟷ centimetres

Fractions

0   1

Starters

Use the grid to answer these.

1   Write the top row in order of size.

2   Write the bottom row in order of size.

3   Write the four central fractions in order of size.

4   Write all the fractions that are greater than $\frac{1}{2}$.

Practice

A Copy and complete these equivalent fractions.

1 $\frac{1}{2} = \frac{\square}{4} = \frac{3}{\square} = \frac{\square}{8}$

2 $\frac{1}{3} = \frac{\square}{12} = \frac{7}{\square} = \frac{\square}{30}$

3 $\frac{3}{4} = \frac{\square}{20} = \frac{18}{\square} = \frac{\square}{36}$

4 $\frac{3}{10} = \frac{\square}{30} = \frac{15}{\square} = \frac{\square}{60}$

5 $\frac{4}{5} = \frac{\square}{20} = \frac{24}{\square} = \frac{\square}{35}$

6 $\frac{3}{8} = \frac{9}{\square} = \frac{\square}{40} = \frac{21}{\square}$

B Copy this line from 0 to 1.

0   1

Mark the positions of: $\frac{1}{3}$ $\frac{2}{5}$ $\frac{3}{10}$ $\frac{5}{6}$ $\frac{1}{6}$ $\frac{1}{2}$ $\frac{4}{5}$ $\frac{1}{5}$

C Place these in order, starting with the smallest.

1 $\frac{1}{4}$ $\frac{2}{3}$ $\frac{1}{5}$ $\frac{1}{2}$ $\frac{2}{5}$ $\frac{5}{6}$

2 0.735   0.8   0.076   0.748   0.75   0.09

3 4.685 kg   4.72 kg   4.7 kg   4.098 kg   4.69 kg   4.681 kg

D Answer these.

1 $\frac{5}{6}$ of 12   2 $\frac{3}{8}$ of 24   3 $\frac{2}{5}$ of 25   4 $\frac{7}{10}$ of 80   5 $\frac{3}{4}$ of 28   6 $\frac{4}{5}$ of 100

E Round these to the nearest tenth.

1 7.48   2 3.55   3 2.92   4 6.34

5 0.75   6 2.19   7 8.45   8 7.54

Challenge

Investigate fractions on a calculator.

Look at the denominators – is there a pattern when changing to decimals?

$\frac{1}{8} \rightarrow 1 \div 8 = 0.125$ $\frac{2}{8} \rightarrow 2 \div 8 = 0.25$ $\frac{3}{8} \rightarrow 3 \div 8 = 0.375$

Try other denominators and record your results.

43

Measuring triangles

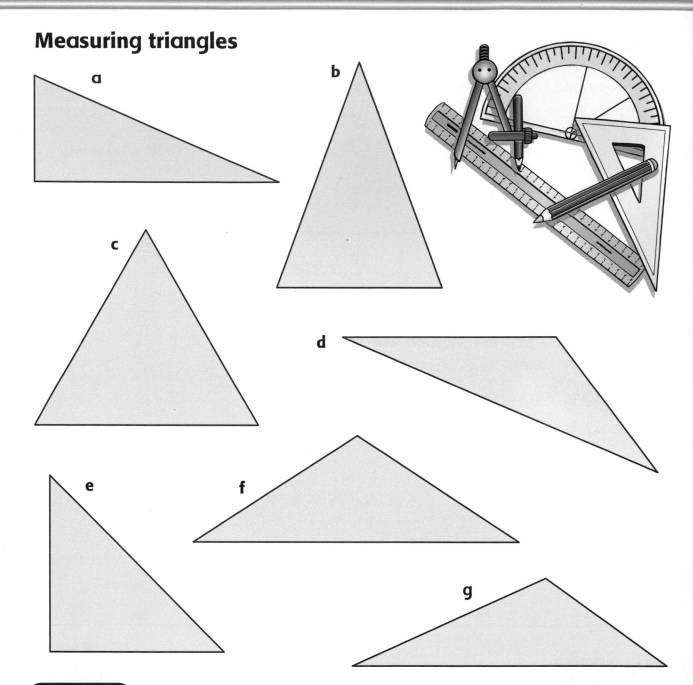

1 Measure the angles of each triangle.

2 Measure the perimeter of each triangle.

3 Choose 3 triangles to copy and draw exactly.

Practice

A

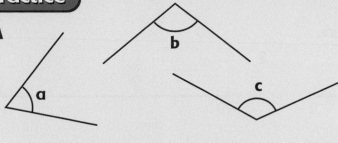
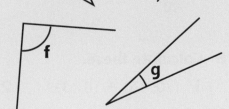
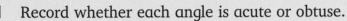

1 Record whether each angle is acute or obtuse.
2 Estimate the size of each angle.
3 Measure each angle.
4 Write each angle in order.

B Calculate the missing angles.

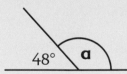
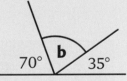
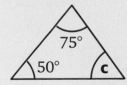
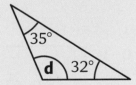

48° a

70° b 35°

75° 50° c

35° d 32°

C What 3-D shapes are these the nets of?

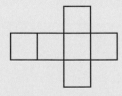
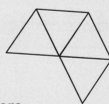
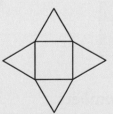
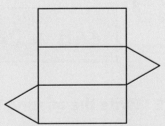

Choose a net to explore.

How many different ways can the net be made?

Challenge

This is a freehand drawing.

Make an accurate drawing of the boat.

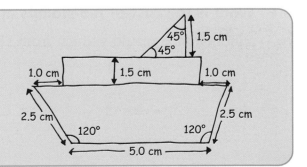

45° 1.5 cm
45°
1.0 cm 1.5 cm 1.0 cm
2.5 cm 2.5 cm
120° 120°
5.0 cm

Review

A Estimate which numbers go here.

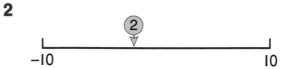

B Calculate these.

  1 $(70 \times 4) + (8 \times 3)$ **2** $(4.8 \div 8) - (27 \div 9)$ **3** $(34 + 18) - (6 \times 4)$

C Write all the factors of 24

D 1
$$47 \times 18$$

2
$$3.9 \times 8$$

3
$$648 \div 24$$

4
$$837 \div 18$$

E Write the missing numbers.

  1 $\boxed{} \div 100 = 0.38$ **2** $749 \div 100 = \boxed{}$ **3** $\boxed{} \div 10 = 0.471$

F What is the cost of 185 stamps at 24p each?

What change would you get from £50?

G Write these fractions in order, starting with the smallest.

$$\frac{1}{3} \qquad \frac{2}{5} \qquad \frac{1}{10} \qquad \frac{9}{10} \qquad \frac{1}{2} \qquad \frac{3}{4} \qquad \frac{7}{12}$$

H What is:

1 $\frac{2}{3}$ of 180 g   **2** $\frac{3}{5}$ of 25 kg   **3** $\frac{7}{10}$ of 120 cm

I Round these to the nearest whole number.

1 4.58   **2** 3.19   **3** 2.84   **4** 1.46   **5** 6.51

J Name these triangles.

1 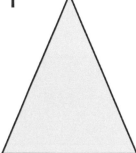   **2** 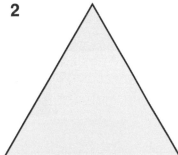   **3**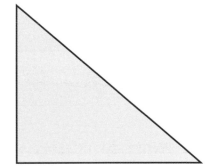

K Measure all the angles of triangle 3.

L What is the missing angle?

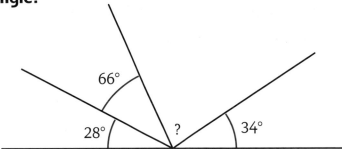

66°   28°   ?   34°

Area

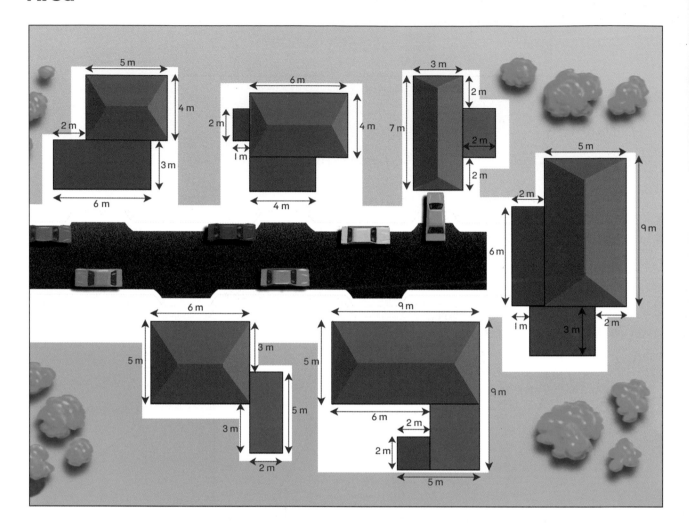

Calculate the area of each house.

Calculate the perimeter of each house.

Practice

A Calculate the area of these rectangles.

1 8.5 cm 9 cm

2 6.4 cm 3 cm

3 12.5 cm 7 cm

4 9 cm 16 cm

5 17 cm 11 cm

Which rectangle has the greatest perimeter?

B Calculate the area of each triangle.

1 8 cm 7 cm

2 6 cm 4 cm

3 10 cm 11 cm

4 9 cm 7 cm

5 9 cm 17 cm

6 6 cm 14 cm

C Draw shapes on a dotty grid.

Each must have an area of 3 square units.

Which shape has the longest perimeter?

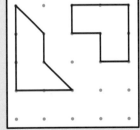

Challenge

Draw circles with a radius of:

 5 cm   2 cm   4 cm   7 cm

Find a way to work out the approximate area.

Measuring mass

Conversion graph: ounces/grams

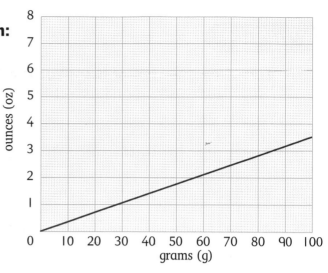

Conversion graph: pounds/kilogram

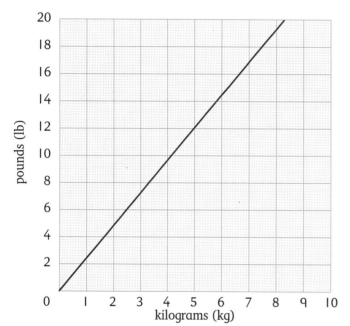

I oz = 28 g

I g = 0.04 oz

I lb = 0.45 kg

I kg = 2.2 lb

Starters

Use the graphs to find these approximate conversions.

Convert these to kilograms.

  1 4 lb   **2** 12 lb

  3 $8\frac{1}{2}$ lb   **4** 14.6 lb

Convert these to pounds.

  5 0.8 kg   **6** 3 kg

  7 6.5 kg   **8** 7.2 kg

Convert these to grams.

  9 4 oz   **10** 2.5 oz

  11 0.6 oz   **12** 3.8 oz

Covert these to ounces.

  13 37 g   **14** 45 g

  15 72 g   **16** 90 g

Practice

A This shows the weights of a group of adults.
Write their weights as decimals.

kg
79.0 ① ②   ③ ④   ⑤   ⑥   ⑦   ⑧   80.0

B **1** 1.75 kg = ☐ g   **2** 3.6 kg = ☐ g   **3** 7.85 kg = ☐ g

   4 0.4 kg = ☐ g   **5** 0.375 kg = ☐ g   **6** 0.15 kg = ☐ g

   7 3900 g = ☐ kg   **8** 1630 g = ☐ kg   **9** 4783 g = ☐ kg

C **Answer these.**

1 How many grams of sugar must be added to 1.38 kg to make 2 kg of sugar altogether?

2 Two marrows weigh 9.36 kg together. If the heavier marrow is twice the weight of the lighter one, how much do they each weigh?

3 There is 4.75 kg of flour in a bag. How many bags are needed for 30 kg of flour?

4 In a vegetable show, two potatoes weigh 1.32 kg and 976 g. What is the difference in their weight?

D **Find the equivalence between metric and imperial weights:**

ounce (oz)   pound (lb)

ton   kilogram

   tonne   gram

Metric → Imperial
1 g → ☐ oz

Imperial → Metric
1 oz → ☐ g

Challenge

Tricky measures – how could you find:

- the weight of a grain of rice?
- the exact weight of an egg (without the shell)?
- the weight of a bike?

51

Adding and subtracting decimals

Starters

Answer these.

1 0.55 + 8.45   2 7.85 + 5.05   3 0.75 + 3.05   4 2.5 + 4.95

5 7.5 + 8.25   6 2.5 – 0.75   7 4.95 – 3.05   8 5.05 – 0.55

9 7.85 – 3.75   10 1.15 – 0.55   11 3.75 + ☐ = 5   12 8.45 + ☐ = 10

13 0.55 + ☐ = 1   14 1.15 + ☐ = 2   15 5.05 + ☐ = 10

Practice

A Answer these in your head.

1 4.81 + 0.7	**2** 2.35 + 1.6	**3** 5.26 + 3.8	**4** 8.31 + 6.9
5 7.34 – 2.9	**6** 1.78 – 0.6	**7** 4.81 – 1.9	**8** 3.62 – 1.8
9 462 + 38	**10** 127 + 84	**11** 394 + 67	**12** 283 + 74
13 614 – 39	**14** 283 – 57	**15** 307 – 48	**16** 538 – 62

B Answer these.

Write three more related facts for each of them.

1 7048 + 1385	**2** 6407 – 2914	**3** 2.38 + 5.76	**4** 7.29 – 3.46

C

1 4835 + 2197	**2** 6705 + 2938	**3** 5174 + 2938	**4** 7152 + 3914
5 7681 – 4139	**6** 8046 – 3127	**7** 4305 – 1817	**8** 8004 – 3795

D

1 16.28 + 8.47	**2** 37.81 +19.48	**3** 49.80 + 17.94	**4** 37.82 + 69.78
5 39.84 – 17.90	**6** 23.80 – 8.35	**7** 31.05 – 26.38	**8** 50.09 – 28.37

Challenge

Make a 4-digit number
Rearrange the digits to make the largest and smallest numbers.
Find the difference between them.
Make the largest and smallest number with these digits.

Find the difference between them.
Continue this: what do you notice?
Try other starting numbers.

9 4 2 1	8 7 2 1	7 4 4 3
– 1 2 4 9	– 1 2 7 8	3 4 4 7
8 1 7 2	7 4 4 3	

Properties of numbers

1	2	3	4	5	6	7	8	9	10
11	12	13	14	15	16	17	18	19	20
21	22	23	24	25	26	27	28	29	30
31	32	33	34	35	36	37	38	39	40
41	42	43	44	45	46	47	48	49	50
51	52	53	54	55	56	57	58	59	60
61	62	63	64	65	66	67	68	69	70
71	72	73	74	75	76	77	78	79	80
81	82	83	84	85	86	87	88	89	90
91	92	93	94	95	96	97	98	99	100

Starters

The Sieve of Eratosthenes.

Put a counter on:

1 all the numbers divisible by 2, but not 2

2 all the numbers divisible by 3, but not 3

3 all the numbers divisible by 5, but not 5

4 all the numbers divisible by 7, but not 7.

List the numbers that are uncovered. These are **prime numbers**.

Eratosthenes was a Greek mathematician who lived from 275 BC to 195 BC. He discovered a method of finding prime numbers of less than 100.

Practice

A **Which of these numbers are:**

56 100 43 32
60 21 81 45

1 multiples of 5?   2 multiples of 4?
3 multiples of 6?   4 multiples of 9?
5 multiples of 3 and 4?   6 multiples of 2 and 5?
7 prime numbers?   8 square numbers?

B **Copy and complete these sequences.**

1 2 9 16 __ __ __ __

2 8 __ __ __ 56 68 __

3 8 19 30 __ __ __ __

4 13 9 __ __ −3 __ __

5 34 28 22 __ __ __ __

6 70 55 __ 25 __ __ __

C **Which of these numbers are:**

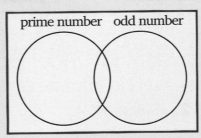

567 261 748 630 196
125 831 217 351

1 divisible by 3?   2 divisible by 4?
3 divisible by 5?   4 divisible by 6?
5 divisible by 9?   6 a prime number?

D **Copy these two Venn diagrams.**

Write the numbers 1 to 50 on each.

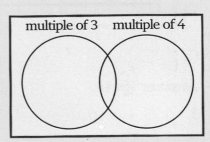

prime number   odd number

multiple of 3   multiple of 4

Challenge

Investigate **prime factors** of numbers

Factors of 12 → 1, 2, 3, 4, 6 and 12

2 and 3 are the only prime factors of 12: they are the only prime numbers.

What are the prime factors of

15 21 30 ? Try others.

Review

A What is the area of each shape?

1
20 cm

14.5 cm

2
7 cm

10 cm

B How many grams in each of these?

1
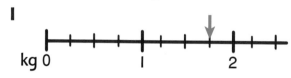
1.85 kg

2
0.325 kg

3

17.2 kg

C What is the reading on each scale?

1

kg 0   1   2

2
g 0   1000   2000

D Answer these.

1 0.25 + 3.16

2 1.48 + 2.7

3 0.6 + 3.85

E

1
47.83
− 39.68
_____

2
31.06
− 18.37
_____

F **What is a *PRIME FACTOR*?**

Give the prime factor of 32.

G **Give three common multiples of 4 and 5.**

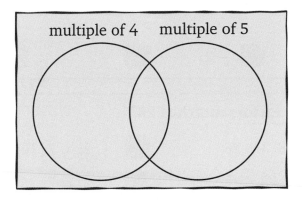

multiple of 4   multiple of 5

H

72   49   153   123   41

Which of these numbers is:

1 a prime number?

2 a multiple of 9?

3 divisible by 3?

4 a square number?

I **Measure these angles.**

1

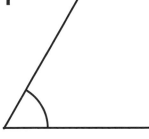

2

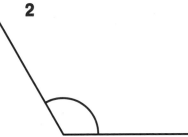

3

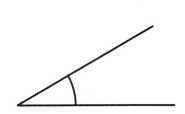

J **Copy this, putting brackets in the correct place.**

$$15 + 7 - 32 \div 8 = 6 \times 36 \div 12$$

Do you remember?

1 **What is the next number in the sequence?**

| 14 | 8 | 2 | ☐ |

 a – 6   **b** – 2   **c** – 0   **d** – 4

2 **Which set of factors matches 28?**

a 1, 2, 3, 8, 14, 28   **b** 1, 2, 4, 7, 14, 28

c 2, 3, 14, 28   **d** 1, 2, 3, 7, 14, 28

3 **Which of these fractions could be in the missing square?**

$$\frac{1}{2} > \boxed{} > \frac{1}{5}$$

a $\frac{3}{4}$ **b** $\frac{3}{10}$ **c** $\frac{2}{3}$ **d** $\frac{3}{5}$

4 **Which of these is an isosceles triangle?**

a

b

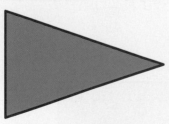

c

d

5 **Estimate the size of this angle.**

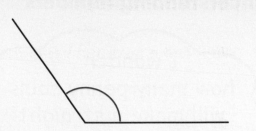

  a 125°   **b** 35°   **c** 270°   **d** 100°

6 **What is the size of the missing angle?**

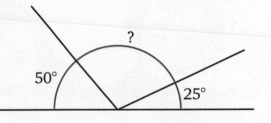

  a 15°   **b** 285°   **c** 75°   **d** 105°

7 **What is the area of this triangle?**

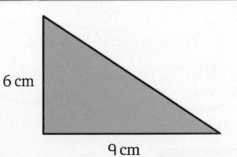

6 cm

9 cm

  a 54 cm²   **b** 30 cm²   **c** 15 cm²   **d** 27 cm²

8 **Which of these numbers is divisible by both 3 and 5?**

  a 140   **b** 225   **c** 365   **d** 530

Check your answers on page 96. ✔

Understanding numbers

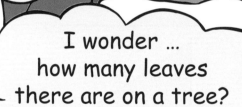

I wonder ...
how many penny coins
will make a straight
line 1 km long?

I wonder ...
how many slices of
bread your class will
eat in a lifetime?

I wonder ...
how many leaves
there are on a tree?

I wonder ...
how many words
there are in a book?

Starters

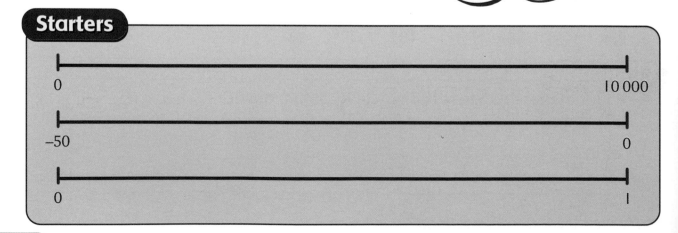

0   10 000

−50   0

0   1

Practice

A Estimate the position shown by each arrow.

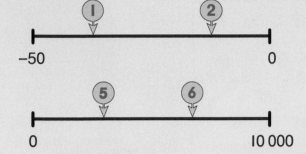
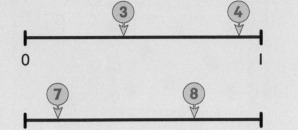

B Round each number.

to the nearest 10

| 1 | 387 | **2** 4245 | **3** 829 004 | **4** 361 296 | **5** 1 000 355 |

to the nearest 100

6 4871   **7** 34 529   **8** 603 550   **9** 214 848   **10** 638 295

to the nearest 1000

11 4500   **12** 6485   **13** 84 493   **14** 792 893   **15** 465 458

C Give approximate answers for these calculations:

1 40.37 − 17.95   **2** 3146 + 87 993   **3** 3.85 × 9.12

4 1093 × 19   **5** (385 − 93) ÷ 18   **6** 29 × (8.8 + 17.31)

7 (9.8 × 4) + 39.61   **8** 83.8 + (2.3 × 7.9)

Challenge

Investigate 1 million   **1 000 000**

How long would it take you to walk up 1 million steps?

Could you lift 1 million peas?

Have you lived for 1 million minutes?

Could 1 million people fit on your playground?

Problem solving

Borgon — 106 tr, 62 tr

Albars — 71 tr, 85 tr

Crill — 34 tr, 103 tr

Droons — 87 tr, 61 tr

Elmid — 59 tr, 104 tr

Aliens measure in trods (tr)

Their money is the yet and the zot
100 yets = 1 zot

Fencing:
62 yets per trod

Zap Seed:
45 yets per trod^2.

Starters

1 Calculate the cost of fencing for each alien.

2 Calculate the cost of putting zap seeds on each alien garden.

Practice

A Answer these using mental strategies.

1 $0.8 \times 20 = \boxed{}$ 2 $30 \times \boxed{} = 15\,000$ 3 $0.3 \times \boxed{} = 2.4$

4 $\boxed{} \times 0.4 = 2$ 5 $6.3 \div 7 = \boxed{}$ 6 $\boxed{} \div 5 = 0.7$

7 $17.6 \div 4 = \boxed{}$ 8 $87 \div \boxed{} = 0.087$ 9 $0.15 \times 0.5 = \boxed{}$

10 $\boxed{} \times 5 = 4.5$ 11 $0.3 \times \boxed{} = 2.4$ 12 $4.2 \times 6 = \boxed{}$

13 $\boxed{} \div 2 = 0.6$ 14 $49 \div \boxed{} = 0.49$ 15 $480 \div 12 = \boxed{}$

B Write remainders as fractions.

1 $48 \div 5$ 2 $68 \div 6$ 3 $43 \div 4$ 4 $93 \div 7$

5 $52 \div 9$ 6 $83 \div 8$ 7 $90 \div 7$ 8 $74 \div 3$

Write remainders as decimals, to 1 decimal place.

9 $84 \div 5$ 10 $37 \div 6$ 11 $69 \div 4$ 12 $83 \div 10$

13 $85 \div 7$ 14 $93 \div 8$ 15 $82 \div 4$ 16 $77 \div 5$

C Divide these by 15   **Divide these by 18**

1 £57.60   2 £42.45   5 £19.08   6 £30.24

3 £144.60   4 £103.35   7 £89.46   8 £135.54

D

1 $\begin{array}{r} 364 \\ \times\ 75 \\ \hline \end{array}$ 2 $\begin{array}{r} 854 \\ \times\ 68 \\ \hline \end{array}$ 3 $\begin{array}{r} 609 \\ \times\ 37 \\ \hline \end{array}$ 4 $\begin{array}{r} 327 \\ \times\ 58 \\ \hline \end{array}$ 5 $\begin{array}{r} 294 \\ \times\ 49 \\ \hline \end{array}$

E

1 $17\overline{)476}$ 2 $23\overline{)897}$ 3 $19\overline{)855}$ 4 $28\overline{)392}$ 5 $34\overline{)714}$

6 $42\overline{)966}$ 7 $31\overline{)589}$ 8 $35\overline{)805}$ 9 $21\overline{)987}$ 10 $48\overline{)816}$

Challenge

Use these digits

Which arrangements produce the
largest and smallest products?

63

Money and measures

	Alex	Ali	Claire	Imran	Kate	Mark	Jenny	Joe	Ann
Age	22	25	20	31	24	26	30	27	29
Height (metres)	1.58	1.68	1.52	1.83	1.75	1.69	1.62	1.80	1.50
Monthly income (£)	1020	985	1108	2480	941	1388	2063	1450	2794

Starters

Calculate the mean average:

1 age
2 height
3 monthly income

Practice

A Answer these.

1 Paving slabs are 96 cm long. A path is made using 12 slabs. How long is the path?

2 If the paving slabs are square, what is the area of each slab?

3 It is 293 km from York to Norwich. A bus travels there and back every day. How far does the bus travel in 1 week?

4 A car travelled an average speed of 73 km/h for a 6-hour journey. How far was the journey?

5 A chef makes 350 sandwiches for a wedding. He expects each guest to eat 4 sandwiches. If there are 83 guests, how many extra sandwiches did he make?

6 Jo swims 1200 metres in a sponsored swim. She swam 40 lengths. How long is the swimming pool?

7 An estate agent's fee for selling a house is 5%. What fee will he get on a house costing £90 000?

8 8000 sheets of paper are put into boxes. If each box holds 745 sheets, how many boxes will be needed?

9 A rope is 6 metres long. How many lengths of 465 cm can be cut from it?

10 A gardener works 9 hours a week for 27 weeks, 6 hours a week for 19 weeks and has 6 weeks' holiday a year. How many hours does he work in a year?

B Make up 'number stories' for these:

1 $157.5 + 38.55 = 196.05$

2 $7.48 \times 32 = 239.36$

3 $68.9 - 3.67 = 65.23$

4 $265.16 \div 28 = 9.47$

Challenge

True or False: The average family has 2.4 children.

Fractions and decimals

$\frac{3}{4}$ 0.667 $\frac{1}{3}$ 0.7

$\frac{2}{5}$ 0.3 $\frac{1}{4}$ $\frac{1}{5}$

$\frac{7}{10}$ 0.125 0.2 0.75

$\frac{1}{8}$ 0.333 $\frac{7}{8}$ $\frac{2}{3}$

0.4 0.875 $\frac{3}{10}$ 0.25

Starters

Write as a decimal:

1 $3\frac{3}{4}$ m 2 $4\frac{1}{8}$ l 3 $7\frac{2}{3}$ m

4 $6\frac{7}{10}$ km 5 $2\frac{2}{5}$ kg

Write as a fraction:

1 6.875 m 2 1.25 kg 3 9.2 cm

4 7.667 l 5 5.7 km

Practice

A Write each fraction as a decimal.

1 $\frac{2}{5}$ 　　　　2 $\frac{3}{4}$ 　　　　3 $\frac{7}{10}$ 　　　　4 $\frac{3}{8}$

5 $2\frac{3}{5}$ 　　　　6 $7\frac{17}{100}$ 　　　　7 $9\frac{1}{4}$ 　　　　8 $4\frac{39}{100}$

Write each decimal as a fraction.

9 0.28 　　　10 3.03 　　　11 4.75 　　　12 8.2

13 0.08 　　　14 9.13 　　　15 5.25 　　　16 3.875

B Use > < or = for each of these.

1 $\frac{1}{2}$ ☐ $\frac{3}{5}$ 　　2 $\frac{1}{3}$ ☐ $\frac{4}{12}$ 　　3 $\frac{7}{8}$ ☐ $\frac{3}{4}$ 　　4 $\frac{1}{3}$ ☐ $\frac{1}{2}$ 　　5 $\frac{3}{20}$ ☐ $\frac{7}{10}$

6 $\frac{1}{4}$ ☐ 0.3 　　7 0.25 ☐ $\frac{2}{5}$ 　　8 $\frac{2}{3}$ ☐ 0.6 　　9 $\frac{4}{5}$ ☐ 0.8 　　10 $\frac{17}{100}$ ☐ 0.2

C Write a fraction that could go in each square.

1 $\frac{2}{3}$ > ☐ > $\frac{1}{3}$ 　　2 $\frac{7}{10}$ < ☐ > $\frac{5}{8}$ 　　3 $\frac{1}{4}$ < ☐ < $\frac{3}{4}$ 　　4 $\frac{3}{8}$ > ☐ < $\frac{3}{10}$

D Write these sets of fractions in order.

$\frac{17}{100}$ $\frac{2}{3}$ $\frac{1}{2}$ $\frac{3}{10}$ $\frac{3}{5}$ $\frac{1}{12}$

$\frac{4}{5}$ $\frac{1}{3}$ $\frac{31}{100}$ $\frac{9}{10}$ $\frac{5}{6}$ $\frac{3}{4}$

Challenge

Use these digits to make fractions which change into exact decimals.

Now use the digits to make fractions which do not change into exact decimals.

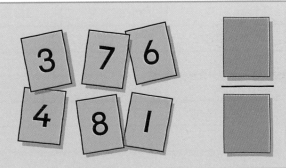

Ratio and proportion

Copy and complete the table.

Item	Price	10% off	5% off	20% off
Computer	£1245			
Monitor	£268			
Modem	£123.80			
Mouse mat	£2.50			
Printer	£208.35			

Practice

A Copy and complete the table.

Fraction	$\frac{7}{10}$	$\frac{3}{4}$				$\frac{7}{20}$			$\frac{3}{5}$
Decimal	0.7		0.6		0.01			0.02	
Percentage	70%			40%			95%		

B Calculate these.

1 25% of 200 g   2 10% of £8.50   3 70% of 5 kg   4 30% of £5

5 90% of 400 l   6 75% of £20   7 5% of 800 ml   8 2% of £65

C Answer these.

1 On a campsite there are 50 full sites. 62% are tents and the rest are caravans. How many caravans are there?

2 A hat costs £18. It is reduced by 20% in the sale. What is its sale price?

3 The price of a car is increased by 5%. If it was originally £12 300, what is its new price?

4 In a survey of 700 cart owners, 60% said they preferred the new 'krunchy cat' catfood. How many did not prefer it?

5 An offer from 'Starbright Windows' is 80% discount on any purchase over £3000. What would be the cost of a set of windows costing £4200?

6 A football team played 30 games. They won 50% and drew 20%. How many games did they lose?

D Talk about ratio and proportion.

Challenge

These are the answers to really difficult percentages.

What could they be?

£6   255   1.5

Handling data

These are the results of a traffic survey in 1 hour.

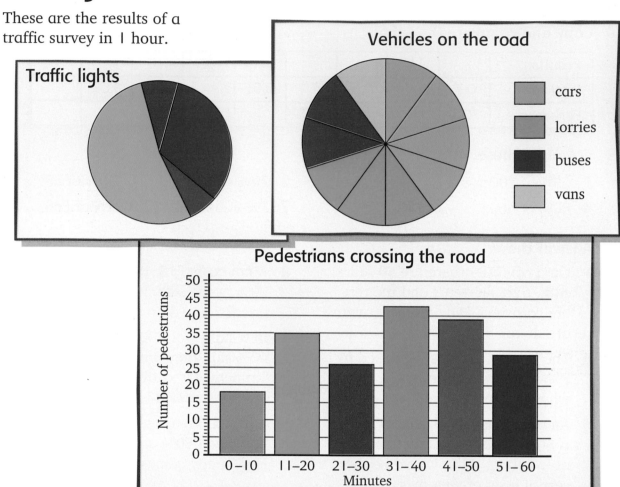

Traffic lights

Vehicles on the road

cars

lorries

buses

vans

Pedestrians crossing the road

Number of pedestrians

Minutes

Starters

Traffic lights

1 What is ⬤ ?

2 What is ⬤ ?

3 If red is 2 minutes, approximately how long is green?

Vehicles

4 What fraction of vehicles were cars?

5 What percentage were buses?

6 If there were 480 vehicles seen altogether, how many were lorries?

Pedestrians

7 How many pedestrians were there in the first 10 minutes?

8 How many were there altogether between 11 and 30 minutes?

9 How many pedestrians were there altogether?

Practice

A 1 What was the most common range of scores?

2 How many children altogether took the test?

3 What fraction of them got between 31 and 40 marks?

4 What percentage of the children got between 51 and 60 marks?

5 What proportion of the classes got fewer than 20 marks?

6 How many children got more than half marks?

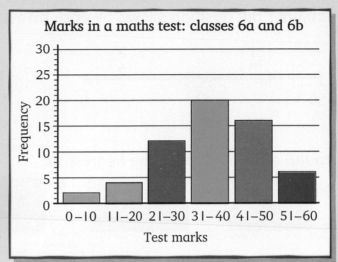

Marks in a maths test: classes 6a and 6b

B School A: 200 pupils

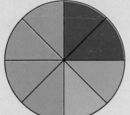

School B: 240 pupils

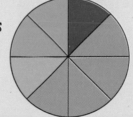

Travelling to school
- cycle
- car
- walk
- bus

Copy and complete these tables from the two pie charts.

School A	Fraction	%	Number
walk	$\frac{1}{2}$		
cycle			
bus			
car			

School B	Fraction	%	Number
walk		50%	
cycle			
bus			
car			

Challenge

Design and draw a pie chart to show how the children in your school arrive at school. How will you find the information?

Review

A Estimate the position shown by each arrow.

−50   0   0   10 000

B Round each number to the nearest 10.

1. 461
2. 3249
3. 47 115
4. 392 644

C Round each number to the nearest 100.

1. 739
2. 4552
3. 68 391
4. 748 261

D Answer these.

1. $19.6 \div 4$
2. $1.2 \div 3$
3. $7.25 \div 5$

E A piece of string is 340 cm long.

How many lengths of 45 mm can be cut from it?

F **Write as decimals.**

1 $2\frac{3}{5}$ 2 $4\frac{3}{4}$ 3 $6\frac{3}{10}$ 4 $9\frac{17}{100}$

G **Write as fractions.**

1 4.25   2 7.35   3 0.02   4 6.8

H **Write these fractions in order.**

$$\frac{4}{5} \qquad \frac{3}{100} \qquad \frac{3}{10} \qquad \frac{5}{6} \qquad \frac{1}{2} \qquad \frac{3}{4}$$

I **Calculate.**

1 40% of £8   2 2% of 300 ml

3 15% of £40

J **Write the missing numbers.**

1 $25\% = \dfrac{1}{\boxed{}}$ 2 $\boxed{}\% = \dfrac{2}{5}$ 3 $12\% = \dfrac{\boxed{}}{25}$

73

Curves

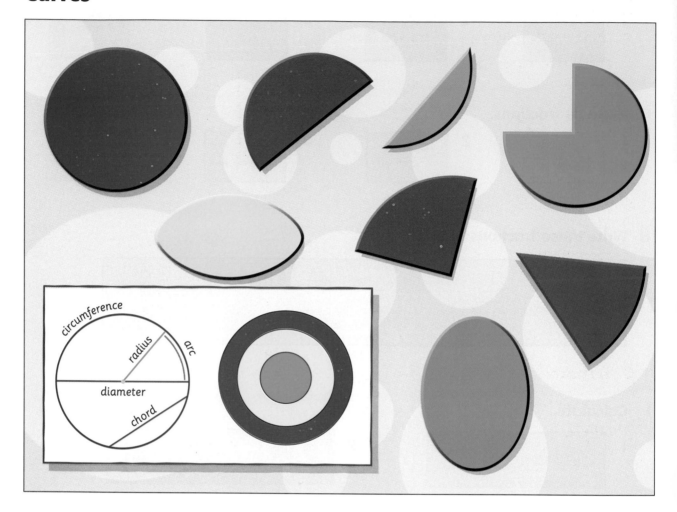

Starters

1   Draw a circle:

with radius 4 cm; with diameter 11 cm.

2   Draw concentric circles with 3 cm, 4 cm and 5 cm radius.

Draw another set so that they overlap. Colour the pattern.

Practice

A Sketch each shape and mirror line.

Draw the reflections.

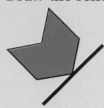 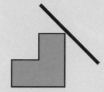 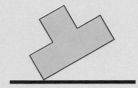

B Copy the grid and shape.

Draw the reflection of the shape in the other quadrants.

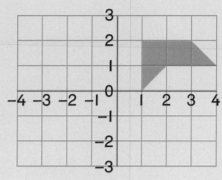

C Translate this shape

3 squares ⟶ right

then

2 squares ↓

down

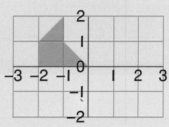

Challenge

Investigate spirals.

This is a 1, 2, 3 spiral, turning clockwise.
Keep repeating 1 square (turn)
2 squares (turn), 3 squares (turn)
Try a 1, 2, 3 spiral. Investigate others:

(3, 1, 2) (2, 1, 1) (4, 1, 3)   Look for patterns.

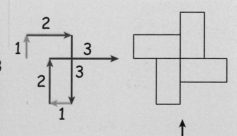

final shape

Solid shapes

These are the five regular platonic solids.

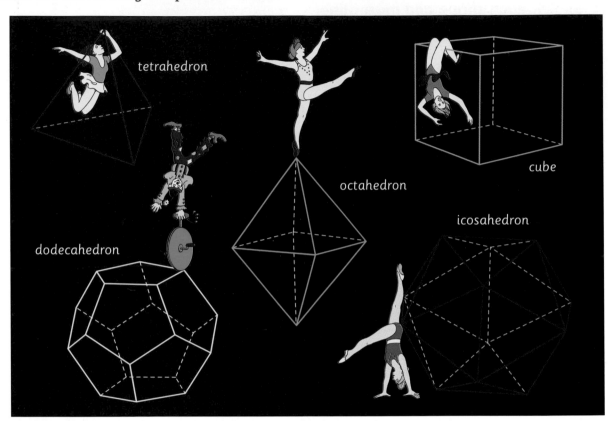

Copy and complete the table.

Name	shape of faces	number of faces
tetrahedron		
cube		
octahedron		
dodecahedron		
icosahedron		

Sketch the net of each shape.

Practice

A Which quadrilaterals are congruent to X and Y?

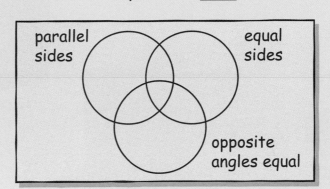

B Sort different quadrilaterals on a Venn diagram like this.

Use shape tiles and then draw up the results.

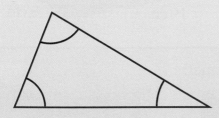

C Talk about.

The angle sum of a triangle is ☐°.

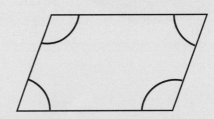

The angle sum of a quadrilateral is ☐°.

Challenge

Investigate intersecting lines.

How many intersections are there from 2 points to 2, 3, 4 ... points?

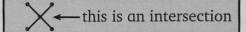

I intersection   2 intersections

Capacity and volume

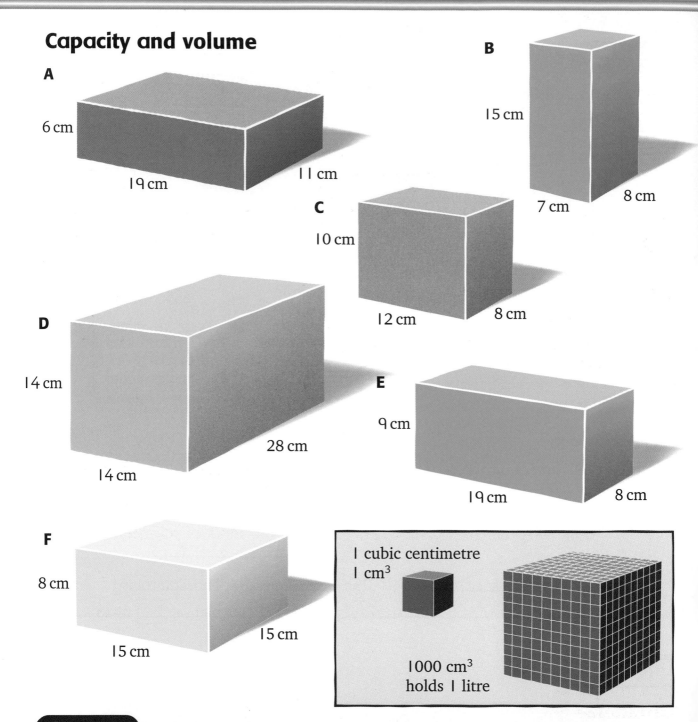

A

6 cm

19 cm

11 cm

B

15 cm

7 cm

8 cm

C

10 cm

12 cm

8 cm

D

14 cm

14 cm

28 cm

E

9 cm

19 cm

8 cm

F

8 cm

15 cm

15 cm

1 cubic centimetre
1 cm³

1000 cm³
holds 1 litre

Starters

1 Which box holds the most?

2 Which box holds the least?

3 What is the surface area of box D?

4 How many cm³ will fill box E?

Practice

A What is the reading on each measuring jug?

1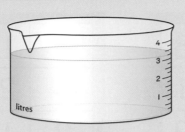

2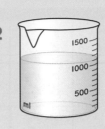

3

B

1 $1.85\ l = \boxed{}\ ml$

2 $4.7\ l = \boxed{}\ ml$

3 $8.09\ l = \boxed{}\ ml$

4 $0.45\ l = \boxed{}\ ml$

5 $0.385\ l = \boxed{}\ ml$

6 $0.205\ l = \boxed{}\ ml$

7 $2800\ ml = \boxed{}\ l$

8 $4780\ ml = \boxed{}\ l$

9 $3620\ ml = \boxed{}\ l$

C Answer these.

1 A full bucket holds 4.6 litres. A full jug holds 0.2 litres.
How many jugs full of water will fill the bucket?

2 A bottle holds 1.35 litres. It is $\frac{3}{5}$ full. How much is in the bottle?

3 A garage orders 80 000 litres of petrol. It sells an average of 2000 litres a day. How long does its supply of petrol last?

4 A 2.2 litre bottle of lemonade is shared between 5 people. Approximately how much will each receive?

D Find the equivalence between metric and imperial units of capacity.

quart   pint

litre   fluid ounce

gallon   millilitre

Metric → Imperial
1 litre → $\boxed{}$ pints

Imperial → Metric
1 pint → $\boxed{}$ litres

Challenge

Tricky measures – how could you find:

- the quantity of water in a raindrop?
- the amount of water in a puddle?
- the quantity of water drunk in a week by your class?

Mental calculation

4	17	25	38
9	11	22	31
1	14	23	39
7	19	30	35

7	14	22	34
4	20	23	38
2	19	25	31
6	17	28	37

5	12	28	34
9	18	21	39
1	15	24	32
8	11	29	36

3	13	21	40
8	20	26	32
5	12	23	35
10	17	29	38

10	15	30	35
6	19	21	33
3	12	27	40
2	16	24	36

6	16	27	37
7	13	24	36
2	18	22	33
9	15	26	39

Starters

Choose a bingo board.

Cover the answers with counters.

Practice

Joke Shop Warehouse

Item	Number in stock	Unit price	Number ordered	Total cost
Coloured wigs	1493	£6.75	45	
Monster masks	5274	£2.83	30	
False noses	71 293	£1.95	28	
Whoopie cushions	694	£4.19	34	
Itching powder	92 146	£1.68	84	
Arrow through head	6843	£3.05	50	
Chattering teeth	10 432	£4.12	29	
			Total	

This is the order form for the 'Jesters Joke Shop' from the Joke Shop Warehouse.

1 Calculate the total cost of each item.

2 What is the cost of the total order?

3 How many of each item are left in stock after this order has gone out?

4 How much more did they spend on wigs than on itching powder?

5 How many items were ordered altogether?

6 What fraction of the order were the arrows?

7 What percentage of the order were monster masks?

8 The total weight of the parcel with all the items is 9.6 kg. If the cost of postage is 32p per 200 g, what will be the cost of sending the parcel?

Challenge

The Joke Shop Warehouse reduces all its prices by 20%.

What will the new prices be for each item?

Functions and formulae

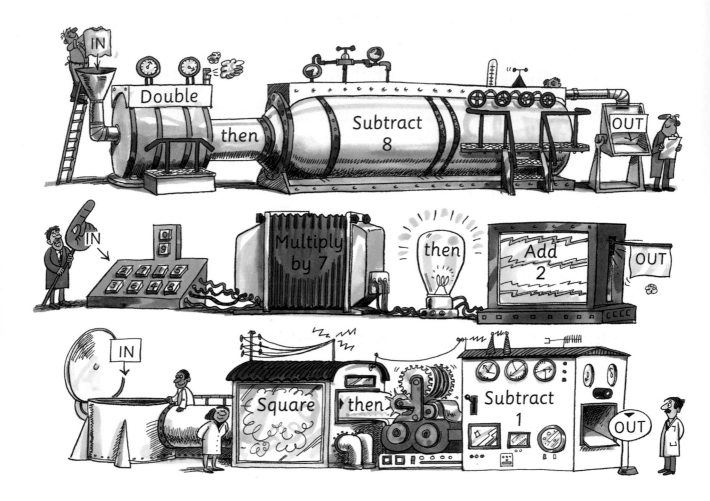

Starters

1 Draw a table or results

In	
Out	

2 Choose five numbers to enter each machine.
Which numbers come out?

Practice

A Which numbers less than 100 include these as their factors?

Show the prime factors in each set.

1 [2, 3, 6, 7, 14]   2 [2, 3, 4, 6, 8, 12, 16]   3 [5, 7, 35]

4 [2, 3, 6, 13, 26]   5 [2, 5, 10, 25]   6 [2, 3, 4, 6, 8, 9]

B Write an equation for each of these.

1 There are 14 people in a lift. *n* people leave the lift. How many are left?

2 The sides of a square are *x* centimetres long. What is the perimeter of the square?

3 David has scored *y* goals in a season. If he plays 18 games, what is the average number of goals he scores per game?

4 Tickets cost £8 each. What is the cost of *n* tickets?

C Predict the next number in each of these sequences.

Write a rule for each.

1 1   3   7   15   ___   2 1   2   5   14   ___

3 6   8   12   20   ___   4 5   6   8   12   ___

5 4   5   9   14   ___   6 12   22   42   82   ___

Challenge

Use rods to make sequences.

Write a formula for each sequence.

Formula
R = 4 × S

Rods (R)   4   8   12

 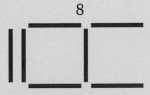 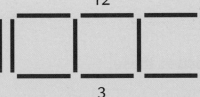

Shape (S)   1   2   3

Review

A Talk about reflection.

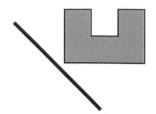 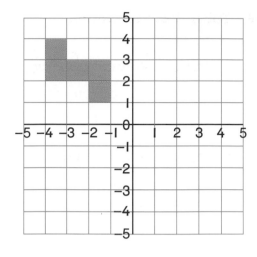

B Talk about these times.

C What are the missing angles?

1

?

34°   41°

2

?   120°

50°   55°

D Talk about these containers.

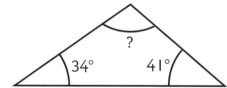 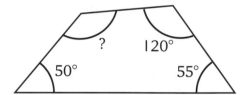

E Answer these.

1 $0.305 \, l = \boxed{} \, ml$

2 $6.35 \, l = \boxed{} \, ml$

3 $3160 \, ml = \boxed{} \, l$

F **Total these amounts.**

£3.74   94p   £12.68

G **What is 40% of these?**

1 200 ml   **2** £8   **3** 1.21

H **Make up word problems for these.**

1 $6.25 \times 18 = \boxed{}$ **2** $(73 \times 4) + 30 = \boxed{}$

I **What are the factors of:**

1 40   **2** 81   **3** 37

Talk about these different numbers.

J **Find the value of *n* in each of these.**

1 $n + 7 = 10$ **2** $3n = 15$ **3** $\frac{n}{4} = 9$

and a final tricky one! $3n - 5 = 7$

Place value

Digits

There are ten digits: 0, 1, 2, 3, 4, 5, 6, 7, 8, 9

Thousands

A shorthand way of writing a thousand is to use k:

examples

3000 = 3k   50 000 = 50k

Commas are sometimes used to separate thousands from hundreds:

examples

3425   86,205   159,238

Multiplying and dividing by 100 and 1000

Multiplying by 100:
move the digits 2 places to the left and fill the spaces with zeros.

Multiplying by 1000:
move the digits 3 places to the left and fill the spaces with three zeros.

Dividing by 100:
move the digits 2 place to the right.

Dividing by 1000:
move the digits 3 places to the right.

Rounding

To the nearest 10:
look at the last digit, if less than 5 round down, otherwise round up.

examples

643 round down 640
38 266 round up 36 270
598 115 round up 598 120

To the nearest 100:
look at the last two digits, if less than 50 round down, otherwise round up.

examples

3346 round down 3300
49 362 round up 49 400
309 650 round up 309 700

To the nearest 1000:
look at the last 3 digits, if less than 500 round down, otherwise round up.

examples

4312 round down 4000
56 809 round up 57 000
283 500 round up 284 000

Millions

millions	hundred thousands	ten thousands	thousands	hundreds	tens	units
M	Hth	TTh	Th	H	T	U

2 000 000 + 400 000 + 10 000 + 3000 + 200 + 10 + 3 = Total: 2 413 243

Number patterns

Multiples

The multiples of 3 are	3, 6, 9, 12, 15, …
The multiples of 4 are	4, 8, 12, 16, 20, 24, …
Multiples of 8 are always even	8, 16, 24, 32, 40, 48, …
Multiples of 5 always end in 5 or 0	15, 40, 65, 80, …
Multiples of 10 always end in 0	10, 30, 140, 200, …

Rules of divisibility

Whole numbers are divisible by:

10 if the last digit is 0	350, 2900, 6730, 2190, …
5 if the last digit is 0 or 5	455, 260, 385, 205, …
2 if the last digit is an even number	244, 8776, 3108, 2330
3 if the sum of the digits is divisible by 3	81, 162, 255, 834, …
4 if the last two digits are divisible by 4	144, 1328, 3640, 2076, …
6 if it is even and also divisible by 3	126, 384, 1056, 3348, …
8 if half of it is divisible by 4	144, 576, 440, 984, …
9 if the sum of the digits is divisible by 9	324, 2052, 5787, 2907, …

Factors

Factors are numbers which will divide exactly into other numbers.

The factors of 18 are 1, 2, 3, 6, 9 and 18	5 is a factor of 5, 10, 15, 20, …
The factors of 30 are 1, 3, 5, 6, 10 and 30	7 is a factor of 7, 14, 21, 28, …

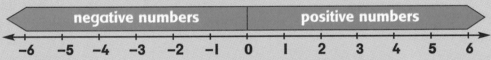

Prime numbers

Numbers which can only be divided by themselves and 1.
Prime numbers up to 20 are

2, 3, 5, 7, 11, 13, 17, 19

Number sequences

When looking for a pattern in a sequence of numbers, look at the difference between consecutive numbers:

```
7      11      15      19      …
   4       4       4       4
```

Square numbers

To make a square number, multiply a number by itself:

$3 \times 3 = 9$ 9 is a square number
$7 \times 7 = 49$ 49 is a square number

Square root

To find the square root of a number, find a number that, when multiplied by itself, gives that number:

$\sqrt{49}$ 7×7 is 49   so $\sqrt{49} = 7$

Addition

Addition can be done in any order

It does not matter in which order you add numbers. Choose the order you find easiest.

examples

$13 + 29 = 29 + 13$

$45 + 93 = 93 + 45$

Knowing doubles

Knowing doubles can help you find other totals.

examples

$50 + 50 = 100$
$51 + 53 = 104$

$46 + 46 = 92$
$46 + 47 = 93$

Quick methods

Adding 9:
Add 10 subtract 1 $74 + 9 = 83$

Adding 19:
Add 20 subtract 1 $112 + 19 = 131$

Adding 99:
Add 100 subtract 1 $253 + 99 = 352$

Adding 999:
Add 1000 subtract 1 $8456 + 999 = 9455$

Adding the tens then the units

When adding TU numbers, try holding the first number in your head and then adding the tens and then the units.

examples

$47 + 36$ $47 + 30 = 77$ $77 + 6 = 83$

Addition and subtraction are opposites

An addition sum can be checked by subtracting.

examples

$58 + 46 = 104$ $104 - 46 = 58$

Breaking up numbers can help add mentally

| 4 | 9 | + | 3 | 7 |

↓ ↓   ↓ ↓   add the tens then add the units

$(40 + 9) + (30 + 7)$ $70 + 16 = 86$

Adding the nearest decade number and adjusting

$56 + 79$ $56 + [80 \text{ then} -1] = 135$

$64 + 52$ $64 + [50 \text{ then} +2] = 116$

Written addition

If the numbers are too big to add mentally, it may be better to use a written method. This is one method commonly used.

```
  574    4 add 8 is 12
+ 218    write 2 in the units
    2    column, write 1 under
    1    the tens column
```

```
  574    70, 10 and 10 is 90
+ 218    write 9 in the tens
   92    column.
    1
```

```
  574    500 and 200 is 700
+ 218    write 7 in the
  792    hundreds column
    1
```

Subtraction

Quick methods

Subtracting 9:
  subtract 10 add 1   73 – 9 = 64

Subtracting 19:
  subtract 20 add 1   137 – 19 = 118

Subtracting 99:
  subtract 100 add 1   481 – 99 = 382

Difference

To find the difference between two numbers, subtract them.

example

64   97   97 – 64 = 33
                                   ↑
                              difference

Subtraction and addition are opposites

A subtraction sum can be checked by adding.

example

86 – 38 = 48   48 + 38 = 86

Subtracting the nearest decade and adjusting

93 – 48   93 – [50 then +2] = 45

81 – 44   81 – [40 then –4] = 37

When subtracting close numbers, count on or back

423 – 418

count on from 418

or count back from 423

The answer is 5

When subtracting, mentally count on using the 'shopkeepers' method'

93 – 58

Count on from 58 to 60
              (hold 2 in your head)

Count on from 60 to 90
              (hold 30 in your head)

Count on from 90 to 93
              (add together 2, 30 and 3)

The answer to 93 – 58 is 35

Breaking up numbers can help to subtract mentally

78 – 46

78 – 40 – 6

= 38 – 6 = 32

Written subtraction

If the numbers are too big to subtract mentally, it may be better to use a written method. This is one method commonly used.

$$\begin{array}{r} 784 \\ -\ 458 \\ \hline \end{array}$$ You cannot take 8 from 4 so exchange a ten for ten ones to make 14.

$$\begin{array}{r} 78\overset{7}{\cancel{8}}\overset{1}{4} \\ -\ 458 \\ \hline 6 \end{array}$$ 14 take away 8 is 6.

$$\begin{array}{r} 78\overset{7}{\cancel{8}}\overset{1}{4} \\ -\ 458 \\ \hline 326 \end{array}$$ 70 take away 50 is 20: write in 2 tens
700 take away 400 is 300: write in 3 hundreds.

Multiplication

Multiplying decade numbers

Multiply significant numbers first then adjust for the tens:

multiply first

$$70 \times 80 = 5600$$

Multiplication and division are opposites

Division is the opposite of multiplication. This can be used to work out missing number problems:

$8 \times ? = 312$

$312 \div 8 = 39$

Multiplying TU numbers by a single digit

Either multiply tens first then units:

58×6

$(50 \times 6) + (8 \times 6)$

$300 + 48 = 348$

or

multiply units first then tens:

$(8 \times 6) + (50 \times 6)$

$48 + 300 = 348$

Approximating answers

Estimate an approximate answer before working out the exact answer, and check that the answer is sensible: 38×63 is approximately 40×60, which is 2400. The exact answer is 2394.

Pencil and paper methods

When a multiplication is too difficult to calculate mentally, use a written method.

$$
\begin{array}{r}
37 \\
\times \ 49 \\
\hline
333 \\
1480 \\
\hline
1813 \\
\end{array}
$$

When calculations are set out in columns, units should line up under units, tens under tens, etc.

Area method

When a multiplication is too difficult to calculate mentally the area method can be used:

68×73

	70	3
60	4200	180
8	560	24

$$
\begin{array}{r}
4380 \\
+ \ 584 \\
\hline
4964 \\
\end{array}
$$

Halving and doubling

For some calculations, halve the smaller number and double the other:

34×8

68×4

$136 \times 2 = 272$

Division

Dividing by 2: halving

Dividing by 2 is the same as halving:

$72 \div 2 = 36$ half of $72 = 36$

Halving odd numbers gives an answer with a half in it:

half of $85 = 42\frac{1}{2}$ half of $97 = 48\frac{1}{2}$

Remainders

These are the remainders possible when dividing by:

6   0, 1, 2, 3, 4, 5

7   0, 1, 2, 3, 4, 5, 6

8   0, 1, 2, 3, 4, 5, 6, 7

9   0, 1, 2, 3, 4, 5, 6, 7, 8

10   0, 1, 2, 3, 4, 5, 6, 7, 8, 9

Approximating answers

Estimate an approximate answer before working out the exact answer, and check that the answer is sensible:
$612 \div 3$ is approximately $600 \div 3$, which is 200.

The exact answer is 204.

Multiplication and division are opposites

Division is the opposite of multiplication. This can be used to work out missing number problems:

$? \div 6 = 42$

$42 \times 6 = 252$

Pencil and paper methods

When a division is too difficult to calculate mentally, use a written method.

This method is developed from repeated subtraction.

$$
\begin{array}{r}
23 \\
6 \overline{)\ 138} \\
-\ 120 \quad (6 \times 20) \\
\hline
18 \\
18 \quad (6 \times 3) \\
\hline
0
\end{array}
$$

Decimals, percentages and fractions

Writing fractions as decimals

Tenths and hundredths can be written as decimals.

$\frac{3}{10} = 0.3$ $\frac{67}{100} = 0.67$ $\frac{841}{1000} = 0.841$

Writing decimals as fractions

Decimals can be written as fractions.

$0.9 = \frac{9}{10}$ $0.85 = \frac{85}{100} = \frac{17}{20}$

$0.77 = \frac{77}{100}$ $0.387 = \frac{387}{1000}$

Per cent sign (%)

A number followed by the per cent sign (%) shows a fraction out of 100.

$35\% = \frac{35}{100}$ $80\% = \frac{80}{100}$

Decimals and percentages

Decimals can easily be changed to percentages by multiplying the decimal by 100.

$0.35 = 35\%$ $0.7 = 70\%$
$0.08 = 8\%$ $0.97 = 97\%$

Percentages can be changed to decimals by dividing the percentage by 100.

$40\% = 0.4$ $28\% = 0.28$ $10\% = 0.1$
$5\% = 0.05$

Fractions and percentages

To change fractions to percentages, make the fraction out of 100.

$\frac{7}{20} = \frac{35}{100} = 35\%$ $\frac{4}{5} = \frac{80}{100} = 80\%$

To change percentages to fractions, make the fraction out of 100 and then simplify the fraction.

$70\% = \frac{70}{100} = \frac{7}{10}$ $45\% = \frac{45}{100} = \frac{9}{20}$

Common percentages

$10\% = \frac{10}{100} = \frac{1}{10}$ $50\% = \frac{50}{100} = \frac{1}{2}$

$25\% = \frac{25}{100} = \frac{1}{4}$ $75\% = \frac{75}{100} = \frac{3}{4}$

$100\% = \frac{100}{100} = 1$ whole

Percentages of amounts

To find 20% of £12, find 10% and double it:

10% of £12 = £1.20   20% of £12 = £2.40

To find 30% of £7, find 10% and multiply by 3:

10% of £7 = £0.70   30% of £7 = £2.10

Fractions

$\frac{2}{3}$ $\leftarrow$ numerator
$\leftarrow$ denominator

Equivalent fractions

Some fractions are worth the same even thought they may look different:

$\frac{1}{2} = \frac{2}{4} = \frac{3}{6} = \frac{4}{8}$ $\frac{2}{3} = \frac{4}{6} = \frac{6}{9} = \frac{8}{12}$

$\frac{3}{4} = \frac{6}{8} = \frac{9}{12} = \frac{12}{16}$ $\frac{3}{5} = \frac{6}{10} = \frac{9}{15} = \frac{12}{20}$

Fractions of quantities

$\frac{1}{2}$ is the same as $\div 2$ $\frac{1}{2}$ of 14 = 7

$\frac{1}{5}$ is the same as $\div 5$ $\frac{1}{5}$ of 65 = 13

$\frac{1}{10}$ is the same as $\div 10$ $\frac{1}{10}$ of 120 = 12

$\frac{1}{3}$ is the same as $\div 3$ $\frac{1}{3}$ of 21 = 7

$\frac{1}{4}$ is the same as $\div 4$ $\frac{1}{4}$ of 44 = 11

Time

Reading time

Analogue time

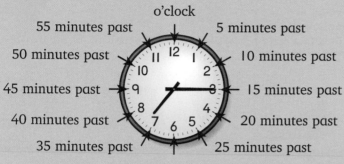

o'clock

55 minutes past · 5 minutes past
50 minutes past · 10 minutes past
45 minutes past · 15 minutes past
40 minutes past · 20 minutes past
35 minutes past · 25 minutes past
30 minutes past

seven fifteen or 15 minutes past 7
- The small hand shows the hour.
- The longer hand shows how many minutes past the hour.

Digital time

shows the hour

shows how many minutes past

seven fifteen (7.15) or 15 minutes past 7

---

a.m. and p.m.

a.m. means *ante meridiem*
It is any time between 12.00 midnight and 12.00 noon.

6.35 a.m.	6.35 in the morning
11.05 a.m.	11.05 in the morning

p.m. means *post meridiem*
It is any time between 12.00 noon and 12.00 midnight.

3.45 p.m.	3.45 in the afternoon
9.20 p.m.	9.20 in the evening

24-hour time

Instead of using a.m. and p.m., 24-hour time goes from 0000 to 2400.

8.50 a.m.	0850 hrs
11.15 a.m.	1115 hrs

a.m. times look the same, but add 12 hours to p.m. times.

1.55 p.m.	1355 hrs
11.20 p.m.	2320 hrs

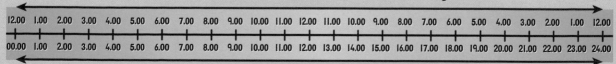

a.m.   p.m.

12.00 1.00 2.00 3.00 4.00 5.00 6.00 7.00 8.00 9.00 10.00 11.00 12.00 11.00 10.00 9.00 8.00 7.00 6.00 5.00 4.00 3.00 2.00 1.00 12.00

00.00 1.00 2.00 3.00 4.00 5.00 6.00 7.00 8.00 9.00 10.00 11.00 12.00 13.00 14.00 15.00 16.00 17.00 18.00 19.00 20.00 21.00 22.00 23.00 24.00

24-hour time

2-D shapes

Number of sides	Name	Number of sides	Name
3	triangle	7	heptagon
4	quadrilateral	8	octagon
5	pentagon	9	nonagon
6	hexagon	10	decagon

Quadrilaterals

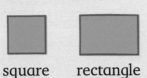

square   rectangle   rhombus

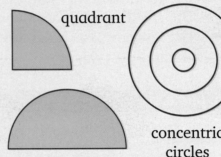

kite   parallelogram   trapezium

Triangles

equilateral   isosceles   scalene   right angle

Circles

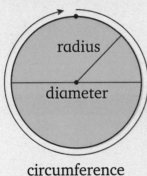

radius

diameter

circumference

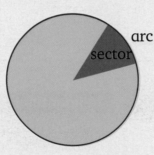

arc

sector

quadrant

semicircle

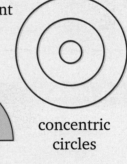

concentric circles

Pentominoes have 5 squares

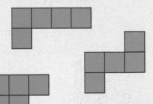

Hexominoes have 6 squares

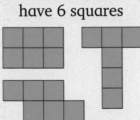

Directions

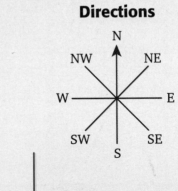

```
        N
NW           NE
W ——————————— E
SW           SE
        S
```

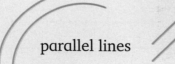

parallel lines

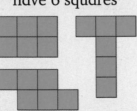

perpendicular lines

3-D shapes

Number of faces	Name
4	tetrahedron
6	hexahedron
8	octahedron
10	decahedron
12	dodecahedron
20	icosahedron

Regular solids

There are five regular solids.

octahedron
(8 equilateral triangles)

hexahedron or cube
(6 squares)

dodecahedron
(12 pentagons)

Net

A net is an opened-out shape.

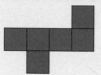

a net of a cube

tetrahedron
(4 equilateral triangles)

icosahedron
(20 equilateral triangles)

Prisms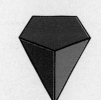

Pyramids

Cone

Cylinders

Hemisphere

Sphere

Do you remember?

Term 1 (pp. 4–5)

1 b	2 a	3 c	4 b	5 d
6 d	7 b	8 a	9 c	10 b

Term 2 (pp. 32–33)

1 c	2 c	3 a	4 d	5 c
6 a	7 d	8 b	9 c	10 d

Term 3 (pp. 58–59)

1 d	2 b	3 b	4 c
5 a	6 d	7 d	8 b